Social Work With Rural Peoples

Social Work With Rural Peoples

Third Edition

KEN COLLIER

VANCOUVER   NEW STAR BOOKS   2006

NEW STAR BOOKS LTD.
#107 – 3477 Commercial Street
Vancouver, BC v5n 4e8   canada

#1517 – 1574 Gulf Road
Point Roberts, WA 98281   usa

www.NewStarBooks.com   info@NewStarBooks.com

Publication of this work is made possible by grants from the Department of Canadian Heritage Book Publishing Industry Development Program and the Province of British Columbia.

Cover by Mutasis Design
First printing, July 2006
Second printing with changes, September 2014

LIBRARY AND ARCHIVES CANADA
CATALOGUING IN PUBLICATION

Collier, Ken
    Social work with rural peoples / Ken Collier. — 3rd ed.

Includes bibliographical references and index.
ISBN 1-55420-020-2

    1. Social service, Rural — Textbooks.   2. Sociology, Rural
— Textbooks.   3. Indians of North America — Social conditions
— Textbooks.   I. Title.

HV67.C64 2006   361.3′2   C2006-902535-5

Contents

Giving Credit Where Credit is Due

Health and Welfare Canada, National Welfare Grants Director-ate helped fund the first edition of this book. The Social Science Federation of Canada also awarded funds from the Social Sciences and Humanities Research Council of Canada. The University of Regina President's Fund provided a grant, and the Faculty of Social Work helped through generous academic work practices at the time that allowed for research and writing.

The three editions are made possible by faith (and expenditure) by New Star Books. For that I thank them very much.

Above all, these folks pressed me ever onward: My wife, Dilys Collier; Joan Turner, then of the Faculty of Social Work, University of Manitoba; Diana Ralph, now of the Faculty of Social Work, Carleton University; Wallis Smith, then of Ontario Ministry of Community and Social Services, who contributed to *Aski-Puko* ("The Land Alone") and other documents referred to in this book and who furthered my understanding of economic phasing and culture; Dr. Harvey Stalwick, Dean of the Faculty of Social Work, University of Regina, from its inception to 1980; Otto Driedger, then Dean of the Faculty of Social Work, University of Regina 1980-1983; Graham Riches, Acting Dean, 1983-1984 and now Director of the School of Social Work at the University of British Columbia; and the Social Administration Research Unit (SARU), Faculty of Social Work, University of Regina.

I was rewarded very significantly in being offered a Visiting Research Fellowship at the Fernand Braudel Center for the Study of Economies, Historical Systems and Civilizations at Binghamton University in New York State in 1993. Immanuel Wallerstein, Director of the Center, made generous provision of resources, time and consultation, as well as access to working sessions of task forces and committees pursuing the research agendas one finds on the website (http://fbc.binghamton.edu). Bea Wallerstein let me share her office and discussed background to the growth of the Center and its idea. Donna DeVoist, the Center Administrative Assistant and Managing Editor, provided a constant supply of key contacts.

Inevitably I will miss some who played a role, but I would like to acknowledge my debt to the following: Cec Allen, Art Baalim, Rod Bishop, Rose Bishop, Ralph Bodor, Sally Bowen, Jim Brady, Peter Brook, Linda Bull, Carmen Burnay, Peter Burns, Lesley Carberry, Ben Carniol, Rosemary Clews, Tom Coghlan, Martin Cohnstaedt, Jo Anne Crofford, Jerry Cross, Doug Daniels, Angus Deschambault, Edward Deschambault, Lionel Deschambault, Murray Dobbin, Tom Farrell, Jerry Fisher, John Flett, Marcel Fosseneuve, Maurice Fosseneuve, Roy Fosseneuve, Mary Hall, Bill Harding, Jim Harding, Brian Hill, Linda Hope, John Hope, Terry Jelinsky, Jennifer Keck, Tony Lloyd, Lloyd Mattson, Dawn McInnes, Brad McKenzie, Clayton Moorhouse, Claude Njimba, Malcolm Norris, Sr., Ron Peters, Ted Phillips, Marcia Pollock, Ron Pollock, Allan Quandt, Roberta Quandt, Berry Richards, Mabel Richards, Verna Richards, Heather Ross, Noel Schacter, Les Senner, Gord Shaw, Karl Stange, John Stobbe, Frank Tester, Dale Tingley, Koby Vanderlinde, Leen Vanderlinde, Marie Whitehead, Maureen Wilson, Tony Wood and Kim Zapf.

Virginia Field Smith edited my first efforts and made the manuscript into a much better document. Her analysis, criticism and rewrite contributed more than mere manipulation of words. Great credit is due her, and the faults that remain are mine. My deep thanks to Lanny Beckman, Julian Beder, Rolf Maurer, Audrey McClellan, Carellin Brooks and Grace Yaginuma of New Star Books for their substantial contributions in their turn to the first, second and now third editions. These are all people who know what co-operation really means.

My long term association with the Canadian Federation of Humanities and Social Sciences and with Athabasca University 1997–2005 rewarded me with academic oxygen sufficient to pursue this research and writing project. Since retiring, time allowed for following the topics involved.

Red Deer, Alberta, Canada
December 22, 2005

Preface

In 1984, the introduction to the first edition began:

There are not many books about rural social work.
Those that do exist usually originate in the United
States of America, where the rural poor, aboriginal
peoples, family farmers and migrant labourers com-
prise those whom social workers will meet beyond
the perimeters of the city. These are the people about
whom this book is written — people of North America
and across the world.

The bulk of professional and academic writing about human services in rural and remote areas tends to be descriptive, in that it catalogues the ways in which services are presented in rural areas. For example, a 1970s era task force on rural practice in Georgia[1] published an overview of features of rural life for social workers to be aware of, as well as the attributes these workers should have. Since then, a few more books and a few journals reached those who study rural human services,[2] but not much in the way of new breakthroughs.

Rural areas and people are still subject to decisions made far away in the economic and political centres. Rural peoples are still separated from these centres by important differences in ways of living, being, seeing and thinking. Income and other gaps between urban and rural people are, if anything, wider than before, and are getting worse pretty much across the globe. The sad fact is that these differences continue to deeply affect how human service workers do their professional work. The publisher, New Star Books of Vancouver, reports that there is still strong demand for this book. That is nice for the publisher and for me as an academic, but it is really an indictment of our social and economic system that the need should still be there, and that the problems of rural peoples remain intractable.

The principal aim of this book is to provide benefit to people working in broadly defined human service organizations in rural and remote areas. If it succeeds, it will be useful to educators, health personnel, agricultural and forest workers, policy-makers and perhaps others. The skills, techniques, values and theories behind social work must relate to the realities of rural and remote life, and meet those realities. Clients of the systems which employ social workers may find it helpful. Rural people have a right to expect human services personnel to understand their situations, to design work methods that are attuned to local peoples. All this is not markedly different from urban demands on human service workers. However, urban life tends to be more homogeneous than life in isolated rural and remote areas. The very purpose of assembling people in cities as a predictable, orderly workforce eliminates many cultural variables and severely constricts others.

Rural social work has wellsprings in social forces and disciplines not usually associated with this profession. Some of that material has surprisingly early roots, dating back more than 100 years. Their theoretical foundations built on community development, child and adult learning and rural culture. While mainstream urban social work built on the familiar disciplines of psychology, sociology and political science, rural social work had piers of support in rural organizing, education extension related to the farm and the rural experience in the health professions, mainly public health nursing. Some of it is North American, some European, some flowing from Latin America.[3]

This book, the product of three decades of experience, research and teaching in rural social work, economics and social studies, rests on an important assumption: that, at least for now, the presence of social workers in rural communities and throughout the organizations to which rural people must relate is unavoidable. Many radicals regard the professionalized services of industrial capitalism as having no honest place among people who are trying to save themselves from a slow death. However, I hope that some social workers will take up a new model (which is in fact an old one) and align themselves with their clients — that they will make a bad system work against itself.

What does a social worker do under such conditions? Can the worker maintain professional standards honestly? The answer is yes. Contradictions within the dominant industrial society are such that a social worker can exploit them to the advantage of the client. Industrial capitalism created structures which a worker with rural people can use — small pockets of money exist to assist in organizing; scattered groups of people support the efforts of aboriginal, farm and other rural people; some bureaucracies are ambivalent enough about their mandates to create programs which can be controlled by citizens; and best of all, conflicts among powers in government and elsewhere create breathing spaces within which rural peoples can gain ground. Although these "institutions of contradiction" can never create freedom from exploitation, they can be used by the people to advance toward specific goals as they are needed. Social workers from time to time have networks of rural organizations which run their own show, to which the workers can refer clients and with which they can align themselves.

Only if social workers understand their positions in their own society — as critics and as those who work for society's transformation — can they approach their work in the exploited society in peace. If they see themselves as traitors to their society as a result of following this critical approach, it is because they identify with its power structures and not with its people. This identification will show through their work, and they will feel torn between two extremes — between trying to make the rule book work and burning it.

A good friend[4] reminded me that the works of the early American anthropologist, Lewis H. Morgan, were used by both Karl Marx and Adolf Hitler. Morgan would likely have had little sympathy for either. The point was well put. I should make my own values and hopes plain. I would be dismayed if this book were used to find more effective ways of incorporating rural peoples into the industrial economy and social relations against their wills. I wrote this book, the product of four decades of experience, to illuminate the relationships between economic phases and the institutions that help to build and maintain them. Social work and other human services are such institutions, and it is essential that practitioners become far more aware of the functions they perform when they work in rural areas. I would like clients and other citizens to know what is happening, and why, so that if they do not like it, they have some basis for action.

This is not a skills book (although I frequently get requests to make it into one). While it is presented as being in part about practice, that practice will be in exercising analytical skills and tools, not in honing particular practical skills. Rural social forms are too varied, even among close neighbours, to use social work skills like a formula. Rural human service workers require an ability to see and to understand what is happening, and then to construct ways of dealing with the realities. That, "simply," is the major job for rural workers, as I see it: interpreting, analyzing, constructing.

That is the way it should be.

I

Introduction

Can social work methods and theories be transferred successfully from the urban context, where they were first developed, to rural regions? As we shall see, the distinct conditions which exist in rural and remote societies call upon the human services worker to become aware of the differences and, in most cases, to change the ways in which helping skills are extended. There is evidence to suggest that some actions may be called for in rural areas that are not presently in the mainstream social work repertoire, but should be.

Conversely, some items in that repertoire will have to be abandoned. The rural social worker must ponder why commonly used social work methods do not work in an aboriginal village or in a ranching and farming region when they have proved effective in the big city.

Social work and industrial society

Whereas the practice and grounding theories of such professions as medicine[1] and law,[2] which predate industrialism, were totally transformed as the industrial state arose, social work is a child of industrial society. Social work developed as a service to the industrial state and exists in order to tend the casualties of the system. Social work is not alone in doing this, of course — various other service disciplines and agencies perform similar functions, directly or indirectly. Wilensky and LeBeaux outline the development of social work as it is found in Western Europe and North America today.[3] Industrial capitalism resulted in the erosion of

support structures in the extended family and kinship systems. The state had to build replacements for those support
structures as the numbers of victims of industrial activities
began to mount. In the process, the state found that the welfare activities it created also could serve to extend control
over the workforce.

In crushing the traditional, custom-oriented feudal relations, industrial capitalism radically altered the daily lives
of the mass of ordinary people. Economic realities transformed cultures as industrialization coloured the social fabric. The change from agrarian feudalism to nascent industrial capitalism altered the way people related to each other.
Among aboriginal* populations of North and South America, Australia and the South Pacific, and Africa, as in sturdy
and isolated communities everywhere, the transition to
industrialism has not fully taken place.

In many of these societies we see today a process experienced over a hundred years ago by European and other industrialized peoples. The relations among rural and remote
peoples reflect the remaining structures of their hunting and gathering or agricultural communities, and often
reflect the tensions and problems caused by increasing contact with industry, or, if you will, the city. Comparing rural
and urban societies frequently resembles the act of comparing pre-industrial and industrial societies. In fact, remote,
mainly aboriginal populations are placed in circumstances
very similar to pre-feudal and feudal peoples during the rise
of industrialization in Europe.

This book is clearly Marxist in conception. That is, it takes
a materialist stance in suggesting that the ways in which
people act and the ways in which their culture is formed and
maintained are based on the interaction between their economic activity and initiatives made possible by the human
imagination. While a Marxist approach has its critics, it
offers analytical tools for understanding social relations
which, in my view, no other theory provides. This approach,

however, is open to distortion. "Vulgarizers," for example, have a tendency to reduce it to an "economic determinist" outlook,[4] which assumes that foragers (that is, hunters and gatherers) always act one way, agriculturists another way, and that a formula for human services can be developed which will apply to all non-urban peoples. While the economics of foraging and agriculture are basic to the arguments presented here, there are, of course, many other elements in the makeup of any culture. Geography, weather, access to resources, presence or absence of animals of burden, religious forms, power relations — the list is long; all affect the way culture and its many functions evolve.[5] There is no inevitable process through which every society, every culture, moves from foraging to agriculture to industrialism, in a forced march, without variance. These processes are particular to each society, are reversible, and may even skip a particular phase.

I chose to avoid cataloguing all the theories and philosophies typically presented in a full social science curriculum in a college and university. Other texts do that. In particular, though pressed to do so, I do not deal with postmodernism, since I believe it has more or less run its course as, at least in part, an anti-Marxist and individualistic set of theories. Many of its proponents from the 1970s or onwards later withdrew from its embrace, and some that had Marxist backgrounds returned, saying that postmodernism is not only wrong on the evidence, but is a disorganizing and demobilizing force, not useful in either professional life or human affairs.[6]

---

* The word "aboriginal" is used here in the current North American sense, meaning those here first, or "first peoples."

2

Economic Phases and Helping Relationships

Theory is a way of explaining events. While a valid theory helps us to make sense of some aspect of the world and categorizes it so we may see its patterns, it is not a carbon copy of the real world. The real world can be full of exceptions, idiosyncrasies and sometimes outright mysteries.

Historically, societies tended to evolve from a period of hunting and gathering to an agricultural economy and ultimately to industrialism. The formal and informal ways in which people before the age of industrialism supported each other, managed their environment, solved social problems and organized themselves politically provide insights into the workings of cultural formations likely to be found in rural and remote areas.

The foragers

Every society started as a nomadic hunting and gathering society. This earliest stage represents a foraging economy in which all people were involved in some way in providing for their subsistence.

Some foraging societies enjoyed richer, more productive environments than others. Weather, terrain, animal life, natural disasters and water resources determined the fortunes of any particular group. People mainly focused on such matters as the progress of the seasons, wind, rain, snow, fire, eclipses, disease and other natural phenomena which had, in fact or perhaps symbolically, some effect on their foraging operations. People were among many natural entities, along with animals and trees, fishes, pests and the elements, which had to coexist in the environment. The concept that people controlled or determined things, as the one kind of creature who interferes with natural events and laws, is foreign to the hunter and gatherer. Interference tends to be expressed symbolically, through religious supplication, for example, rather than through the agency of individuals or groups of foragers "doing something" to their surroundings.

Although scarcity was sporadic, and affected all, and although luxury was rare, hunting and gathering societies were far from being grim, harsh or unhappy.[1] The interdependence of every individual in the society was not only a daily necessity, but a daily comfort. Every foraging society existed in a communal matrix of relationships which promoted its survival.

Each person was expected to perform virtually all the basic tasks required for living, and if there was specialization,[2] it was only because personal preferences could be tolerated in good hunting times, or because the environment was rich in produce. At other times, as during war, natural disaster, scarcity or pestilence, each member had to perform many functions.

As in all societies, foragers ensured that social obligations were recognized and enforced — in their case by strategic marriages, clan alliances, formation of taboos and placements of children in the homes of relatives. The formulas were strict and characterized high levels of social development.

In foraging societies the kinship system is of primary importance in the reproduction and maintenance of the social forms. Kinship is a social web of varying size in which people relate to each other largely on the basis of their work in order for the society to survive. Local geographic features, climate, food and other resources determine the number of people in a kinship system, and exactly how they will relate.

Broadly speaking, the kinship system — often referred to as a tribe — consists of those people born to the local society who are identified as those who participate in the survival activities of that society.

In harsh surroundings, such as the Arctic, the number of people in a kinship system is small, since the amount of territory required to garner all the resources needed per person is very large. The amount of travelling to cover the required territory limits the number of people in such a kinship system. It is not practical to take hundreds of people on treks of hundreds of kilometers on foot. In general, the larger the group, the slower the travel. More lush and productive surroundings, for instance the South Seas, make it possible for many more people to live on the terrain and water within reach of the population. Travel, even for large numbers of people, can be undertaken, there being security in the knowledge that food and shelter can be found or made with less effort and delay than in severe cold or dry conditions.

Kinship systems, though they vary in size, have certain features in common, due to their worldwide function of providing a livelihood from the land for foraging peoples. Though there are variations in how such systems work internally, in broad features they share enough in common to be considered one kind of formation.

Although natural parents had an important role as the procreators of the society, children belonged to the people as a whole, rather than just to the biological parents. Adults or older children who had little or no blood relationship often served as de facto parents or caregivers. Some cultures were extremely simple, others complex. Their languages tended to be more internally logical and consistent, with fewer rules and exceptions than we find in industrial society languages. One might expect the languages of hunting and gathering people to have a smaller lexicon, since they were, on the whole, unwritten. This, however, is not necessarily true. Since language not only reflects culture, but carries it as well,[3] it should not be surprising, for example, that the languages of foraging societies often contain many words for kin relationships that have fallen into disuse in industrial society. Also there are no modern equivalents for the many specific names given to natural phenomena like snow, water or wind. The cultures of aboriginal peoples were likewise attached firmly to the necessities of survival. No leisure classes lived off the work of others. Significant events, such as war, were carried on in ways consistent with survival requirements. Wars were not fought indiscriminately. If war was fought in earnest, it was almost never for conquest of territory, the taking of slaves or captives, or simply for property. In many cases war was a way of forcing internal cohesion among factions or clans who otherwise might be causing strife inside the society. If opponents could be frightened or bluffed away, all the better. Even when actual battle took place, the clashes were usually on a small scale, with relatively little loss of life. Wars engaged only the combatants, not the whole population. Widespread killing or injury of non-combatants was almost non-existent. Often skirmishes consisted of either slightly injuring an enemy, or touching him without injury and running away, signifying great bravery. Occasionally slaves were taken or captives hauled away to revive a declining population.

Decision making among hunters and gatherers was virtually population wide. Each person knew what part he or she could play in any project, and spoke for himself or herself only. Rarely was anyone made the "representative" of another. Those appointed or selected to head projects like the hunt or building a lodge were "chiefs" of that activity in that they could better accomplish that activity than anyone else. Their power or authority over others rested on their knowledge and ability. Privilege did not accrue to a chief, only responsibility. The chief of the hunt, for instance, was not given a share, typically, until all others received their food. Men or women could become chief, and in the oral traditions of the many hunting and gathering peoples around the world there are tales of male and female chiefs accomplishing great deeds.

Elders, on the other hand, were recognized as advice givers. They had knowledge and asked good questions. Their role was to be a source of insight, inspiration and connection with the gods or the forces which ruled life. Age had little to do with being an elder. The abilities of an elder were bestowed on someone, not because he or she sought such abilities, but because the person had been fated to have them. The ability to perform the functions of the elder often came to the elder in the form of a dream, vision or revelation, some-times spontaneously, sometimes as a result of fasting, of temporary isolation from other people, of taking drugs, or by other means to establish contact with the source of know-ledge. There are accounts of elders' abilities being received gradually or without awareness until the ability was finally revealed by a deed.

Neither chief nor elder was seen as a political post. Politics — the representation of one by another, or the power of one group or class over another — did not come about until the rise of agriculture. Chief and elder served, and did not rule. Nor did they try to persuade, but rather tried to encourage and support the persons to carry out their life work well. Personal belongings, art objects and other encumbrances of wealth were few because nomadic existence precluded the transportation of excess baggage; nor did the necessities of survival allow for the making of portable wealth. The lar-ger scale art of nomadic people is normally located on rock faces, or in bone, stone or wooden artifacts constructed for specific purposes — brief entertainment, entreaties to the gods or information about the territory. For instance, the inukshuk in the Arctic guide travellers to the camp. Rock face pictures (pictographs) may tell who lives in the area, what is grown or eaten, or show animals, fish and birds or other items. Smaller art pieces might be necklaces, rings, earrings or other personal adornments.

To varying extents, a foraging economy survives today among North American aboriginal peoples. Some places, such as in the Arctic, were until recently almost unchanged from their original form. In dramatic contrast to the dominant economies around them, small segments of these aboriginal societies continue traditional patterns of hunting and gathering, kinship obligations and their intimate attachments to the land, albeit under fierce and constant pressure. Many foraging societies which were previously forced from the land-based or water-based economies are now trying to regain those ways of life through court contests and occasionally through extra-legal manoeuvres, such as occupying the land, using the resource without permission, or blockading roads or rail lines.

The relatively egalitarian relationships in foraging society can be contrasted with the statuses enforced by governments. The chiefs on First Nations reserves today are unlike the chiefs who attained their position through their prowess or knowledge. They are chiefs in the sense known to industrial society, which means they have authority over others in a way not recognized in the old society. This is revealed by the language many Indian bands use to describe such chiefs. Since their role is essentially that of dealing with government officials, the name often given them in the local dialects is "fake-chief."

Though there is debate about stratification among the people of First Nations, much of what is thought of as strata is imposed from the outside through government influence or fiat. Band councils, committee structures, bureaucratic arrangements and various financial privileges largely originate outside the band itself. There were clans whose statuses appeared to differ, but these differing statuses seem to have had critical functions in the mutual survival of the community. This type of inequality which social workers find so worrisome is not nearly so important as those caused by government or other forces.

Likewise the differences between people on First Nations reserves and those in cities, as well as differences between Treaty Indians and other aboriginal peoples, are largely created by government law and policy — some say created on purpose to divide aboriginal people from one another, to force their assimilation, integration or disappearance.

Many orthodox economists and others present the foraging economy as a "primitive" way of life, in contrast, for example, to agricultural or industrial economies, which are called more "advanced." This is not only an incorrect judgement, but also carries a heavy cultural message. Protagonists of this view frequently see hunters and gatherers as "simple," itself a word carrying all sorts of implied meanings, such as slow-witted, innocent or childlike. But foraging societies, as is true of every economic system and its attendant culture, represent a human response to real conditions. If the society is to survive, it must develop sensible and useful responses. People may not be conscious of the pattern of these responses, nor their reasons, but they work to keep themselves alive.

Explorers and traders from Europe came to the New World and to many of the South Sea Islands, where people hunted and gathered for a living. They adopted the foraging ways of the people in order to survive long enough to discover how these people and their resources could be exploited. Traders and explorers learned from the local people how to live with the environment, there being no other way to obtain food and shelter.

In areas where agriculture and industry are still not feasible, nomadic hunting and gathering remains as sensible as it ever was. The foraging economy and the cultural expressions which accompany it are merely varieties of response to life situations which still exist today. On the whole, however, foraging as a way of life has been damaged severely by the intrusion of the industrial periphery into the territories where hunting and gathering has been the pattern. There are few regions left where the quest for resources — strategic interest in the land or sea or other factors — has not brought outsiders into the worlds of foragers. Foragers do not have much defence against the machinations of the global industrial economy, and the social results staggered local hunters and gatherers.

The agriculturists

To present the agricultural phase of economic development as an "advance" from hunting and gathering is incorrect. The activity of growing crops is generally assumed to be more complex than that of hunting and gathering, but it is not. Crop cultivation makes the food supply more reliable and daily living more possible in circumstances when land access is restricted or decreased. In North America, migrating nomadic peoples gradually discovered that they could harvest some natural crops (grains, fruits, berries) each year, and that with husbandry they could influence the outcome of these harvests. In addition, powerful neighbours or natural disaster frequently limited the land available, disrupting wide-ranging gathering and forcing the adoption of agriculture as a means of survival. Others discovered that certain animals, fowl, fish and shellfish could be domesticated, harvested or aided in their growth by conscious agricultural pursuits.

An agricultural economy requires entirely different survival tasks from those of a foraging economy. As people take up more permanent residence, housing and living patterns change. New knowledge is created and old lost as people shift from finding plants, animals, fuel and shelter in the wild to dealing with the complexities of weather, soil, water, planting, fertilizing, harvesting and storing. Such complications cannot be left to chance, since the interplay among all of the elements of agricultural life is critical to the results. Rules and enforcements grow in number and become ways which ensure continuity of the society.

The development of agriculture brought cultural change. Written language began to develop. Art became decorative and was often used to bestow status on the owner through the invocation of the power of the gods, demons, spirits or other beings depicted by the art.[4] Occasionally art would illustrate a vanquished foe. Art pieces became possessions and, along with other natural or manufactured articles, were displayed, kept as a status symbol, or traded. As agricultural activities expanded and became more complex, technology became more sophisticated. The handheld stick was replaced by a hand-drawn plow, which eventually was harnessed to a beast of burden. Individual wealth began to grow unequally as efficiency at producing agricultural harvests varied. What we now call capital was first acquired in agricultural societies as surplus wealth — machines, storage bins, corrals, repair facilities, houses and more land. The more successful agriculturists purchased labour when the operation grew too large for the family to run it alone, and in this way even bigger surpluses were realized from the hired labour and additional land.

The first major difference between foraging and agricultural economies lies in the presence of reserve produce among agricultural societies. Foragers rarely put away food sufficient to survive long periods without hunting and gathering, although, of course, many foraging societies had methods of storing food (like berries, meat and fish) so it would not spoil, and could be kept buried below the ground like in pemmican bags, or dried, smoked or salted. This is true both because of their nomadic existence and because crops are not harvested in a cyclical manner. In foraging society no one can build up a surplus to last into the indefinite future. If a family should acquire a surplus, they do not keep it to themselves to build up the capacity to get even more — they share it. Foraging society understands its relation to survival in ways which would not allow such differentiation. However, agricultural society may suffer a disaster, perhaps a drought or flood, and is able to use its reserves to tide it through lean times; thus the edge of hunger is pushed back. The owners who possess reserves in their storage bins sell to those who do not, collecting payment from them in more fortunate years. Inequalities become visible. In ways different from agricultural societies, foragers must always be conscious of their fragility, interdependence and equality before the elements.

People in agricultural societies relate to each other only partially according to their labour. There are now social relationships based on new situations. When the rich pass along their capital holdings, it is to their own offspring, who live as a part of the family and who witness the agricultural processes. Young people learned to look after crops and animals, to fertilize the earth and to recognize signs of the seasons. When the old had to pass on the land, the need arose for an orderly, predictable transfer of property to the next generation. Relations of the younger to the older generation became of prime importance. Whereas in a foraging economy the young often lived with any number of older relatives to learn the ways of the people — often moving several times from home to home during their youth — in agricultural societies, succession and the passing on of land presumed very different and particularized relationships between generations. The patrilinear family came into being. Only the children specifically identified by the father as his and his wife's would receive the land and other property, while other offspring in the community would have no claim under the laws developed to support these conventions.[5] The inherited authority over land evolved into inherited ownership of land, and the governing of that land for agriculture was transformed in time to governing for all purposes. "West-centred" interpreters of history recognize that stage, especially in European history, as feudalism, or feudal agriculture.[6]

Extended families that did not own much worked for others. Moral and emotional support was drawn from the family network. The owning classes, upon whom caring responsibilities had now fallen, donated additional assistance as charity. The church opened other avenues for charitable giving, for both rich and poor. In addition to many other social and political connections, the owning classes and the churches provided resources to carry out the helping function and to enforce social relations. Religious specialists practised and refined this role, which expanded further in the industrial economic phase of most societies.[7]

The agricultural phase gave birth to institutions like the church, education, the army and other specialized agencies, which were separate from the everyday lives of people. Each institution had its characteristic relationship with various segments of the economy. The relation of each to foraging peoples was naturally quite different from the relation to agricultural (and industrial) peoples. For foragers, these new bodies were intrusions from the outside, not a part of their own culture or economy.

Industrial society

As agriculture developed, those owners who possessed a greater share of the surplus had more capacity to produce than the poorer people, and thereby had the means to exploit land and labour more efficiently and to survive unfriendly elements. This was a direct outcome of the invention of more efficient machines — of the discovery that, for instance, animals like oxen could pull heavier plows than men or women could. As machines evolved in size and complexity, the knowledge needed to manufacture and maintain them became more specialized. As one example among many paths, blacksmiths evolved into machinists, then into engineers. Eventually the landowners in agricultural societies extended their ability to produce beyond agricultural goods to hard goods like machines. As these industrial activities emerged, there was an even greater need for surpluses in both agriculture and industry. The economy, in shifting to a new stage, took a quantum leap. New rules applied almost everywhere, based on industry's appetite for capital and labour.[8]

What happened to the helping function of agricultural society during the shift to industrialism? People who owned large amounts of capital in the form of buildings and machinery for direct production (or for money to lend) were very busy at a new specialty — money management. The need for profit removed any possibility of using time for charitable endeavours. Nor did the many institutions that were set up to support the new complex social and economic relations have time for helping. This duty of society increasingly fell on government, which in the Western democracies still has the job of trying to deal with the conflict between capital and the people. So, as European and colonial states became industrialized, the governing authorities, entrenched with the aid of armies and laws, made arrangements to help those whose ability to survive was impaired in some way.

In industrial societies, specialists in helping are paid. Charitable institutions, such as the church, were the first to develop these specialists. Later they were formally employed by the government and government-funded agencies set up specifically to provide services. The government assumed the responsibility for handling the inevitable casualties of the new economic order — people who were being driven off the land in order to service the industrial sector. Government frequently intervened to prevent confrontations between those dispossessed of the land and the owning classes.[9] In addition, it was important that those people — who could be friends or relatives — not create a drain on the valuable production time of workers.[10]

The emergence of agriculture from ages-old nomadic, foraging society was logical and perhaps foreseeable, in places where agriculture was at all possible. Aboriginal North American societies developed several non-nomadic variants of agriculture. For example, some bands harvested the seacoast or rivers, watched over and looked after the acquired resources — shell beds, spawning grounds, etc. However, in areas where agriculture or its variants were not possible, such as in the far north or in mountainous or desert areas, societies remained nomadic. If they have not already been destroyed, their economies even today remain tied to the land, and their cultures are different from those found around them.[11]

Finally, many regard the movement from agriculture to industry as logical because the competition between the emerging classes forced society toward accelerating production, accumulation of surplus, and spiraling capital requirements.

Industrial expansion and the need for orderly transfers of power — a relatively easy task where a population was fairly homogeneous and approximately at the same phase of economic development, and more painful where it was not — led to the growth of the modern state. The industrializing trend drove urbanization of the population, reordering agriculture and growth of far-reaching trade patterns, transportation and communications. Traditional cultural assumptions and ways of living had to adapt in hugely distressful ways to the demands of industrial life.

There are many countries, of course, whose populations are not homogeneous, whose industrial workers are separated from agriculture, and whose indigenous populations remain as foragers in remote areas. In these countries agricultural and remote areas are increasingly attractive to industry as sources of raw materials and energy, and as opportunities for capital investment. Canada is one such nation, Brazil another, the Philippines yet another. Some African countries exemplify more homogeneous economies and cultures, yet even there people may be subjected to the "human services" designed to force a rapid transfer to industrialization. Whatever the form of the contest between traditional cultures and industry, the problems of transferring helping services from urban to rural and remote settings are vast and complex.

Foraging and agricultural economies — whether in the Canadian North, the Amazon Basin, Central Africa or Polynesia — all relate to the industrial countries in similar ways. The effects of encroaching industry on the local population are similar. Efforts to "develop" the rural and remote areas of the world to fit into the social and economic webs of industrial capitalism conform to a handful of similar patterns.

Many influences determine whether, and when, a society forages, farms or manufactures. Some societies shifted from foraging to planting to industry in that order, which is the traditional route explained by the theory so far. However, some societies foraged, shifted to agriculture, then returned to foraging. After the Spanish reintroduced horses to North America, some aboriginal people began hunting bison and other big game on horseback, leaving a developed agriculture behind. Even though in many areas agriculture was possible, many North American aboriginal people remained foragers due to belief systems, traditions, methods of colonial control or aboriginal political structures. Sometimes, for example, the technology was absent, preventing the transition from hunting to growing.

Underdevelopment and the social worker

The relation between the dominant industrial capitalist state and remaining foraging and agricultural peoples who exist within it is the key to a full understanding of the problems faced by rural human service workers. The theory proposed here will aid the person working for the government, in industry or for a charitable institution to understand the nature of social work and to try and ameliorate the direst effects of industrial society on rural people.

A chronological description of the evolution of rural and remote societies presents the rural/urban relationship in one way. Another way is to view these differences in terms of the economic relationships between them. There are important theorists[12] who describe the connections between advanced industrial economies and those referred to as developing (or underdeveloped) economies. Their theories, which focus on "metropolis-hinterland" relations (or "centre-periphery," or a number of other similar phrases), suggest that underdevelopment, far from being an accidental result of unequal strength, luck or ability on the world market, is instead a relationship purposely designed to transfer value from the less developed economies to the industrial nations. The peripheral economies, besides being good sources of raw materials, form a specific role in the international capitalist economy that helps to boost profit margins when openings for investment and profit making begin to wither in the mature central economies. Relatively powerless social groupings have their daily, and often lifelong, realities determined by these economic forces. The agencies responsible for these economic relationships exist not only in underdeveloped countries, but in advanced countries as well, where inequalities exist between developed and less developed regions. In North America the industrial cities, by this argument, extract surplus value from the rural parts of the continent, and the imbalance between the metropolis and hinterland is designed to maximize this transfer of value.

What are the characteristics of underdevelopment? Samir Amin's Unequal Development outlines the relationships between centre and periphery as follows:

1. The pattern of transition to peripheral capitalism is different from the pattern of transition to central capitalism (a crucial notion that counters the belief that underdeveloped

areas have the same avenues for development open to them as did London, Boston or Montreal). Development often means the ruin of craft skills, but without replacing them by industrial production. Subsequent investment does not correct these setbacks.

2. Periphery development causes three distortions in the local economy. First, the underdeveloped economy produces exotic goods for the central (developed) market at lower wages, since the remote economy cannot match the productivity of the centre at the same wages. Second, rapid growth in the service and support sectors also occurs, as industry does not grow fast enough to provide jobs for those thrown out of the crafts by industry. Finally there is a tendency toward "lightness": heavy industry does not locate in the periphery, nor can the peripheral economies find the capital to finance and build the industrial base themselves.

3. The profits on foreign capital rapidly leave the underdeveloped country and go to the central capitalist economy.

4. The periphery lacks the means to combat the monopolies and multinationals.

5. Peripheral regions exhibit the same internal features — extreme unevenness in the distribution of products as well as in prices and wages. The local economy suffers due to its role as supplier of the central economy rather than to the needs of the local people. Thus, as Amin terms it, the economy is disconnected or disarticulated. Regional industry cannot cooperate or mesh with adjacent industry, transport, communications, service or other networks in order to reduce costs, as occurs within the central industrial economy. The whole peripheral economy is dominated by the centre.

6. A changeover to production geared to the needs of local people is blocked.

7. There is a tendency toward heavy state involvement in the peripheral economy due to the special burdens placed on the peripheral area while undergoing limited industrialization. Heavy intervention by the state and frequent actual

takeovers by the state reflect the necessity of extraordinary measures to achieve this distorted industrialization. Partnerships between government and corporations, loan guarantees, occasionally even military oppression of workers, are used to force the pace of industrial growth. Government takeover often occurs.

Acting in concert, these processes create the classic condition of underdevelopment, a type of development subordinated to the needs of the central capitalist economy rather than to the needs of the local population. This underdevelopment does not happen accidentally, nor does it take place solely as a result of policy decisions of "evil" central monopolies. Underdevelopment is the result of a continuing need for capital accumulation, a need which finds fewer and fewer opportunities in the central economy for either resource extraction or investment. Neighbouring, and even distant, countries are subjected to the dictates of the central economy. In this contest for resources and means to accumulate capital, all countries, including the socialist countries, are engaged. There is no international socialist economy; world trade is still capitalist, and almost all economic activity is now governed by that fact.

Development strategies at the point of decision

Efforts to become a developed economy vary — depending on resources, labour, transport and the like — but all countries or regions share the necessity to decide how development will take place. Will the country or region yield to pressures by the monopolies to become part of international capital accumulation, or will it opt for self-sufficiency? The latter course is fraught with serious risks — economic, and in some cases military — but it represents the only path to national or regional independence. This is not a free choice. Development needs funding, and the decision to go along with funders' requirements has certain unavoidable outcomes that are not always obvious at the time the choice is made. Sources of money for large-scale development projects are relatively few. The International Monetary Fund, the World Bank, the World Trade Organization, foreign aid from rich nations, and large corporate financial holdings are the most obvious sources of international borrowing. Leaving aside the blunt economic interventions of multinational corporations, areas soliciting development funds have to meet a number of requirements to qualify for the huge sums needed for development. Among the requirements are order and stability, sound economic management and accounting, and organizational and governmental capacity to manage the project.

In practice these development ventures mean, among other things, stricter control of political opposition, the unions, the universities and financial processes.[13] They mean cutbacks in social spending (health, welfare, education) to guarantee repayment of loans and to pump up capacity to generate production. They almost always mean increased spending by the developing country or region out of its own tax base for improved transport and for enlarged social control measures (the police, the army and increased jail capacity). Many of the requirements decrease the ability of the subject economy to make its own decisions, to work toward its own goals or to protect itself and its citizens from outside interference.

Internationally, resource-rich countries with largely rural populations have trouble meeting the requirement for credit qualifications, restructuring society and government to mesh with the needs of international capital. Guillermo O'Donnell reports on the process: the Bureaucratic-Authoritarian state is a reaction to popular political activity which stems from dissatisfactions caused by the lack of development — poverty, inequality and repression.[14] Development requires that popular political activity be brought under control in order to satisfy possible lenders. Social quiescence is difficult to accomplish because such periods show many signs of economic crisis — inflation, declining national productivity, flagging investment, the flight of capital, balance of payments deficits, among others.

Keeping civil discontent under wraps is no small chore; society and government must be prodded, indeed molded, to contain the discontent so as to assure financiers of their security and profits. The controls begin as a response to such requirements. Whether by election or coup, the state, which functions to assure capital of security and growth, takes action to deactivate the popular sector. Unions are either bought off, co-opted politically or repressed. The civil service and professions fear for their incomes and job security. The small owning class is threatened by state action, which favours international capital. The indigenous capitalist sector, although the new arrangements pose significant threats to its interests, often shows enthusiastic support for "rationalization" of the economy. Much change is evident in the personnel who run the state and the economy. Those aligned with the large international corporations (often former or even current employees) begin to assume positions of authority and control. Movement of senior planners and bureaucrats back and forth between the corporate and government sectors becomes obvious.

The state — to remove the threat to local capital and to attract international capital — must guarantee order and stability, i.e., the predictability of the regime. Public debate, and especially public action through strikes, demonstrations, work slowdowns and the like, must be done away with. Tariffs against foreign products must be removed, and subsidies for local capital die. These measures display both the efficiency of the developing economy and the weakness of local capital in the development process, thus further measures are needed to attract international capital.

This adds up to delivery of control over the economy into foreign hands, out of sight of the news headlines. Conscious development of a dependent or underdeveloped economy is well in train. This process takes place gradually and involves serious contradictions for the local owning class, many of whom now wish to attach themselves to the big international money markets without bowing to international control. The historic "moment," usually extending over some years, occurs when the society in upheaval excludes its members from national decisions and simultaneously opens the gates to international finance. During this period the state apparatus seems deaf to the needs of its working citizens and its own sectors of capital, and creates wide swaths in its economy for international capital to occupy.

Once this process has been exposed to the public, as it must be in time, the state faces new problems. It must now present itself as the expression of national will and allow no others to challenge its right to speak for the population. Other claimants are offered jobs within the structure, are bought off with money or power (important positions within the unions and party machinery are often occupied by the same people), or are actively repressed through the courts or through military and police action. At this point local capital must again be courted, because local presence is the only element which can provide the ideological and political support needed by the state to deflect popular discontent. The entry of local capital into the underdevelopment process is defined by two main forces — its own power to recruit support from the popular sector and its weakness before the state and international capital. The state carves the local owning class into new shapes, trains it to act in accordance with the plan for development, and offers it a gratifying new chance for glory and profit. Local capital now takes on its new role as a public and patriotic supporter of foreign capital and is closely allied with foreign interests.

Combatting underdevelopment

In most rural areas it is both possible and crucial to avoid this sequence of events. One can fight the process of becoming an underdeveloped economy. Even when elements of local political and economic power are being incorporated into the process, there is still a stage to come. The final joining of state, foreign capital and local capital has not taken place. Opposition is still alive, and effort to convert debate and struggle into internal, party-dominated and government-run forums is far from complete.

Concerted action can cause foreign capital to hesitate, to waver, and at this point such stalling can have considerable impact. Public debate, unwillingness to yield to those behind corporate and government doors, strikes, slowdowns, public interference with the ability to carry out business — all these put the brakes on underdevelopment, though the obedient media will almost inevitably cast these acts as a dire threat to the community.

Every effort to enhance the ability of citizens to resolve their problems, capture their history and future, and make their own institutions will be another obstacle on the road to underdevelopment.

Mainstream commentators claim that developmentalism has run its course — it's over and done. Rural peoples know from experience that is not a fact. Their lives and resources continue to be claimed to meet largely urban industrial and financial goals. Energy, minerals, timber, water and workers are siphoned away from rural areas for those purposes. Development merely became something new and negative as it adopted neo-liberal forms and practices that impact rural people in ever more destructive ways.

3

Social Work in Industrial Society

Churches, members of religious orders and private agencies that engaged in charitable acts toward the poor and downtrodden were the forebears of social workers in industrial society. The personality of early social work was molded by its work in the settlement houses of urban ghettos filled with the discarded and marginalized people of a disintegrating society. Today, however, social work, which used to be carried on within massive government programs or within large agencies funded primarily through the tax base, are overbalanced by private helping agencies on a fee-for-service basis. Social work has changed from an activity of the church and charities into a profession similar to other major professions in industrial society. In the process a major shift in orientation occurred within the helping organizations: from advocacy for the poor to administration of social services and personal therapy treatment, the profession's new perception of its functions reshaped its theories and practices. Social work incorporated the values of industrial society and became a tool in the development and maintenance of Western European and North American capitalism.[1] (It should be noted that this depiction is true also for other helping professions such as psychiatry and psychology.)

The problems social workers deal with are characteristically those that impair a person's functioning in everyday life, which often means not being able to play a productive role in the social and economic life of the society. Poverty programs nearly always aim at getting the maximum number of people back into the workforce, though there are growing numbers of government programs that recognize some people may never work again, and thus use income security as a payoff for them to stay out of the workforce. Counselling programs usually seek one of two things — improving a person's ability to function in a job, or in a family disrupted by economic distress, marital discord, parent-child problems or "mental" illness. "Physical" illness, of course, falls under the care of other professions and agencies. The family of industrial society is the nuclear family, A central concept in the body of social work writing. It is nonetheless a relatively new structure, a product of the industrialization of society² which has quite different impacts on its members than did earlier forms of society.

Certain milestones in the early development of social work, well discussed in the literature, bear repeating here as they are related to the ability of social work to operate in non-industrial settings.

After the religious orders provided the original impetus, the expansion of helping took two somewhat different turns. Radical political movements in America and Britain exerted social pressures for reform and sometimes revolution, and broadened the base of helping efforts beyond the religious orders. The political left and the religious orders, for different reasons and with different ends in mind, were concerned about poverty and growing unemployment in the inner city. Activists opposed to the exploitation of the enormous population of urban industrial workers began to mobilize the poor, those denied justice, those mistreated by state and private institutions, and those needing help because of miserable living and working conditions. (The term "state" is used here in its broadest sense, to include all the institutions, governmental and non-governmental, which help to maintain the power relationships in any society. These include the police and military, education, media and the church.) These early secular social workers organized people so that they might claim their rights here on earth; the church tended to set its sights on redemption in the afterlife. In Britain, reformists channelled most of their efforts into administrative tinkering, on the assumption that if the helping system could only be made to work, then everyone could live and work in harmony. More radical workers were sidetracked into ever more convoluted administrative wrangling and did less and less actual organizing of the poor and downtrodden.

In the United States the history of social work was quite different. By 1914, and certainly after World War One, public support for social work was beginning to dry up. The owning class had second thoughts about people who organized the poor, associating them with anarchists and other radicals intent on inflaming workers against public order. At the same time, inside the growing field of social work, there were many who preferred not to spend their lives dealing with the wretched and the poor. The work, in other words, was becoming institutionalized, and the profession's class composition was changing. Some social workers wanted to take their work off the streets. They sought to legitimize the organizing and helping efforts of their newly forming profession within the rapidly growing social and health services network.

When the work of Sigmund Freud was introduced into the United States, social work found just such a legitimating mechanism. He offered an analytic system which would take social work off the streets, away from the efforts of organizing the poor, and place it side by side with such already established professions as medicine. Ignoring the more dynamic and radical aspects of Freudian thought, social workers like other professionals were captivated by the suggestion that human misery might be primarily psychological in origin and that, even more appealing, it could be categorized as an illness, diagnosed and treated. As the exciting insights and revolutionary concepts of Freud were appropriated by bourgeois society and reduced to their most deterministic levels, psychoanalysis and psychotherapy became subdivisions of medicine. Social work in the United States attached itself to the medical model, styling itself as "the doctor's colleague."

As the field of publicly funded social services grew, social work combined the British and American models into an institution jointly responsible for dealing with individuals in distress and for keeping the social order. Competition between the two images — Herr Doktor and administrative functionary versus the Social Worker, as an organizer of the poor and agitator for social change, presented an easy choice for funders.

Social work continued to concern itself primarily with the working, producing individual client rather than with the social and economic context within which the individual lived. The additions to its historic and recognized repertoire of social group work and community organizing (or development) reflect this same primary concern and try to render services to individuals in groups, or to individuals organized into more or less functional communities of interest — workers, homemakers, alcoholics. Both types of social work reflect the industrial roots of the profession as the assemblies of clients tend to be categorized by assigned roles in industrial society, rather than, for example, by kinship patterns or geographical proximity. Even community organizing reflects the industrial organization of society — it zeros in on changes in industry to which communities must adjust. (Frequently community organizers try to recapture the helping attributes of kinship-like relations, without an actual return to kinship, or attempt some sort of communal problem-solving, without a commitment to communal relations. Examples of such attempts might include co-operative housing or mutual aid organizations like daycare.)

Social work as an industrial institution

Social work found its niche. It became one of the institutions that help to maintain and advance the industrial economic and social order. Proven now are its powers to enter the mainstream of professional helping and to carve out a territory for its actions and theories. It expanded that territory through eclectic borrowing from other professions and through being flexible about its boundaries (both major strengths, which at times in other professions have been weaknesses). Social work establishes its power bases in the cities; it knows the terrain and relates easily with other institutions after decades of practice.

Social work in agricultural areas, and especially in more remote areas where neither agriculture nor industry exists, is still at a primitive stage. No seminal theoretical works are yet available for rural social workers. Rural social workers are left with the choice of either 1) transplanting urban social work to the country or 2) trying to alter — often covertly — the practice of social work so that its impact on rural and remote peoples will not be as malevolent as the impact of industrial society upon them. The first choice for social workers is the rule, the latter the exception.

What happens when urban social work is taken to rural and remote areas? Its effects, when applied to a different culture rooted in a different economy, are often harmful, however well intentioned. "Protecting" children who live in remote villages by spiriting them off to a foster home in the city may be observant of the law, but it ignores human realities in the settlement and in the kinship system of the community. Frequently the social worker carrying out such a plan has no knowledge of the helping system which might exist in that village.

Some results of transplanting urban social work are patently ridiculous. Only with a sense of wonder can we respond to a "mental health team" flying into a small remote settlement and carrying on their "clinic" as if they were still in an office in the suburbs. The social worker, psychologist, psychiatrist and nurse conducting a case conference on a patient under these circumstances are seen for what they are

— an imported "city slicker" sideshow. The introduction of counselling or protection services by setting up strict office schedules in farming communities or aboriginal villages simply will not work. At the very least, rural and remote social work demands a pace of operation consistent with country life. Great numbers of rural and remote people have no experience with offices other than to be summoned to them for some kind of trial or criticism (perhaps the school principal's office, the police station or the nurse's clinic). An office almost never means anything other than tension or trouble, a circumstance that will not be reversed by the sheer good will of a social worker between nine and five o'clock.

Even more disrespectful is the idea of searching for symptoms of psychosis in a remote villager when there may be perfectly reasonable cultural explanations for his or her behaviour. (This is not to argue that mental illness does not exist in rural areas. There are crazy farmers and crazy aboriginal people.) There is great controversy over the accuracy of psycho-diagnostic procedures in an urban setting. Across cultural lines the risk of misdiagnosis is multiplied many times.

When many of the referrals to the social worker come from other transplanted institutions — such as school, police or public health — the social worker is immediately seen by the client as further evidence of the industrial penetration of the rural area. Nothing makes the relationship of the social worker to the industrial institutions so plain as to see urban social work in operation out of its element, where it is unprotected by the trappings that give the professions their status and legal sanctions.

The most pronounced ill effects are found where foraging economies still exist in some form, where cultures are most different from urban culture. Those areas in transition to agriculture are also in the midst of the cultural shift that accompanies economic change. Agricultural areas are less damaged by the entry of industrial institutions than foraging cultures are, yet the impact can be seen and felt.[3]

Social workers who perceive that basic cultural differences exist, and who attempt to alter their practice in a rural context, will confront many problems that require analysis. How much of the foraging life still exists? To what extent are the local people being assimilated, acculturated or forced into the industrial mold? In agricultural areas, are farmers engaged in non-market agriculture for their own use (for example, in parts of India, Africa, Malaysia), are they in the stage of hacking a marginal market agriculture out of the bush (as in some parts of rural America or Australia), or are they trying to finance a multi-million dollar agribusiness, as in the Canadian prairies? While sorting out the facts and effects of each situation the rural social worker faces a sizeable task of self-adjustment. At the same time, the task demands practical, creative and analytical realignment. It would be nice if the "pure" foraging community or non-market agricultural community existed. One could run tests on it, research it, measure it. But most such communities have long since disappeared. That notwithstanding, as a general rule the more distant from industrial society, the greater the adjustments social workers will have to make in the practice of their trade.

4

Generalist Practice: The Best Option

Historically, the field of social work relied on three specific methods or specialties. Casework with individuals, social group work and community organization (or community development) were the classic divisions within the profession. Other methods used by smaller segments of the profession are social work education (practiced by faculty in university and college professional schools of social work), administration and research. All six of these methods emerged with the evolution of social work as an established discipline and became sanctioned in laws and licensing as well as in agency practice. Their presence is largely a reflection of the growth of social work on its urban base.

More recent developments in the field led many to criticize the continued division of the field into specialties. Generalist social work practice offered an answer to this fragmentation. Beginning in the 1960s, pressure to increase the relevance of social work to contemporary social issues and conditions led some to take up the challenge of reform.[1] Generalist practice is not merely a "supra-method of practice that incorporates various specific methods or combines casework, group work and community work."[2] Proponents of generalist practice have had to reformulate the theoretical bases of social work, and reformulate the practices that arise from such changes. Though development of the generalist approach did not stem directly from the challenges of rural social work, its application to rural areas quickly became evident.

Generalist social work is founded on a theoretical approach different from that of specialist practice.[3] The generalist approaches each problem or issue by estimating the possibility of solution from many vantage points. The generalist considers problem solving on many levels, across a spectrum of conceptual and practical approaches, and pursues any avenue that may be productive. It is not a specific approach, like casework with its theoretical bases. The generalist enters each situation ready to tackle an individual problem, a neighbourhood issue or a political contest. Generalists consider it proper to select whichever approach or approaches will produce the best result, and may engage in all of them.

The generalist is eclectic. Psychology and sociology are adopted as useful disciplinary foundations, but history, political science, economics, anthropology and linguistics as well as behaviour and education theory, among others, are drawn from as appropriate. Though such an approach seems to suggest that the social worker might try to be "all things to all people," that is not accurate. Rather it is an approach that chooses to use many foundations on many societal levels, rather than just a few. It offers a range of extra resources which may lead to the resolution of a problem. The practitioner may make or not make referrals depending on the advantage to be gained by either choice.

The approach suggests a readiness to take on a broad gamut of human problems. This informed flexibility is adaptable to the nature of the work of many rural people, for example, farmers, fishers and hunters. Generalist practice also recognizes that many of the categories of social problems defined by the specialist practice of urban social work do not reflect conditions in rural regions. Many rural problems just do not break down that way and are interconnected with other problems and issues. Rural relationships generate many rural social problems that cannot, and should not, be forced into the industrial social science discipline-based definitions of urban social work practice. If a client develops what is normally seen as a "health" problem, it may be not only advisable but necessary for a social worker to deal with it. Merely because an issue has habitually been seen as falling within the sphere of "education" is no reason for a rural social worker to retreat from it. In fact, since resources in rural areas are usually scarce, a social worker who declines to work on a problem because it falls outside of his or her specialty would, in effect, be denying service altogether.

Aside from one practical advantage of the generalist approach — that it reduces the number of people needed to render services — it has been noted that in a range of situations a single helping person is often more valuable. Rural villagers find it strange and wasteful if a person has only one specialized skill, since one's life cannot be organized around one single activity in the normal course of events. Furthermore, a large influx of outsiders upsets the social mechanisms of a small village. Relationships are changed between and among the villagers, and the internal balance of interrelationships comes under strain. Anyone who has gone to a small town for a few days soon becomes aware of the efforts the people make to deal with the new presence. First, the newcomer is greeted, but perhaps in an aloof manner; under watchful eyes, gradually he or she is incorporated into some segment of the community. The newcomer is something of a celebrity for a time, and many stories circulate around the town about the reasons for the newcomer's being there. The testing of the newcomer's sincerity, purposes and commitment goes on over a period of time — usually a week or two, but that may be extended if the people are occupied by the requirements of the season of freeze-up or breakup, seeding or harvest, summer fishing or winter hunting. Finally an accommodation is made. Although the pressure seems to be only on the newcomer, too many of these incursions place a great load on the ability of a small town or kinship group to adjust.

All cohesive and working communities have ways of helping their members in distress, and many of these are still strong among rural people. Generalist social workers are best able to discover these helping relationships because of the broad conceptual bases generalists work from; they can borrow from many useful sources to engage methods, skills and groupings that will incorporate the strengths that exist. Generalists also have a better capacity to exercise on-the-spot judgement about the best analytical tools and models. A generalist social worker has an enhanced ability to appreciate interdisciplinary approaches, cross-cultural possibilities as well as non-professional and para-professional opportunities for helping. Helping mechanisms that exist in other economic phases and in other cultures are, in general, as potent as any of the "approved" methods the social worker may import.

Here is an example of generalist social work practice:

The social worker, alerted to problems of school attendance and undernourishment, visits the children's home. The worker finds an unemployed father who drinks heavily; the mother expecting another child; a teenage daughter wanting to leave for the city; and several older children who visit the home from time to time to drink, take drugs, eat any food available and generally sponge off their parents, who appear unable to afford or manage such visits in any orderly or disciplined way.

The social worker can intervene in family planning if that is an issue for the family. Counselling can be provided concerning nutrition, school attendance and the problems of the teenage daughter. The social worker could offer either individual help connected with employment or undertake community work to see if year-round employment might be arranged for the family members and others in that predicament. Organizing recreational programming among the community members might make it possible to find other places for the relatives to spend time, lessening the burden on the parents. This could also be extended to benefit other families facing the same problem. It may be pos-

sible to find financial resources for the parents in the
public financial assistance programs. Directing mem-
bers of the family to opportunities for work in other
parts of the region, or even further away, could be pos-
sibilities — even providing transportation or helping
with applications for grants to move to where there is
new work. The generalist takes advantage of practical
opportunities, such as arranging for materials for the
purpose of house repair while the person is otherwise
unemployed.

In these ways generalist social work departs from orthodox practice. The social worker was able to see inter-agency,
cross-disciplinary, multi-level openings for helping.

While generalist practice may seem to oblige the social
worker to take on every facet of every problem, it has the
advantage of setting up cross-disciplinary contacts with
other professionals in which the sharing of opportunities
becomes commonplace. Such coordination need not over-
burden the clients. Rural practice eventually produces professional relationships that are open, co-operative and col-
laborative, in which efforts often provide multiple outcomes
which benefit many people.

Generalism also encourages non-professionals to engage
in problem solving, since the barriers between professional
and non-professional are broken down as frequently as those
between professionals. Rural areas are ripe for the development of volunteer, para-professional and peer helping mechanisms across the broad range of interventions possible.

After the highway was built near the town, packaged
consumer goods became readily available. Previously
villagers threw scraps out the door of the house, and
animals would carry the bones, crusts, peels and other
edible pieces away. Since the arrival of the highway

was not accompanied by a garbage collection service, the practice of throwing the new sort of garbage out the door resulted in health hazards of many sorts — a breeding ground for disease; metal and glass shards which regularly injured animals and people. In addition, the arrival of consumer goods brought the nomadic life of the people to an end. They stayed in their houses year round — houses which had been meant originally as trapping cabins for winter use only. The villagers could not keep the unpeeled logs and rough floors clean with the goods they had at hand. In a very short time, nearly everybody in the village contracted tuberculosis — it spread quickly from house to house, from adults to the young.

A first effort to end the cycles of TB, injury and dirt was to bring a wheelbarrow, rakes, shovels and hoes to the village. One family agreed to work on cleaning up the hill below their front door. I helped, raking cans and bottles, paper and plastic diapers off the hillside. The priest brought his truck to remove the refuse. We drove load after load down to an empty basement, the scene of a house fire some years before, and dumped the garbage into it. (The basement often filled with water in the spring and had claimed three children through drownings.) Other families made rough rakes from tree boughs. Pieces of plywood became shovels.

The priest's truck drove back and forth for days, filling the basement with garbage. A passing bulldozer owned by a natural gas exploration company was commandeered into covering the hole with earth. The priest had a fund — until then never used — which paid for materials to convert some basically sound buildings into houses, and I authorized payments to the priest to replenish the fund for further building. As soon as each house was ready, we burned down the log house

so that no new family could occupy it and thus expose
themselves to the TB infesting the logs. Burning houses
is not usually legal, but the village did not have a well-
developed set of local bylaws on this subject.

While generalist practice suggests a wholeness in which the social worker may shift from method to method, from strategy to tactic, and from discipline to discipline, the generalist can gain from taking the problems and solutions to pieces and examining what can happen in a variety of instances. As an example, the village secretary, though the position is empowering, may in fact be experiencing debilitating personal stress from marital discord or financial difficulties. The generalist social worker may turn to personal counselling for the secretary while, at the same time, slipping the suggestion to the village councillors that a raise in pay would help things along. In addition, by careful reorganization, the secretary's responsibilities and power may be shared; the social worker may try to include both councillors and citizens in the decision-making process.

A chief of a First Nations band may have authority over the use of farm equipment, and may misuse that authority. The band council may be ineffective because of widespread drinking and lack of information, which is under the chief's control. Rather than a frontal attack on the problem, the social worker may help to organize an alcohol treatment program based on aboriginal cultural foundations, knowing that a long-term solution will pay off better than a short-term confrontation, which the social worker may well lose. Alcohol treatment through a local Alcoholics Anonymous always involves discussion of people's problems, and thus opens the opportunity to deal with the issue of the farm equipment from the vantage point of solutions rather than confrontation with entrenched power. The generalist invents holistic ways to solve problems through refusal to be bound by disciplines or narrow job specifications. In rural areas such limitations almost always prove counterproductive.

The generalist vision is one which provides the social worker with a variety of responses to any given problem. He or she may pick one or more at various levels, while borrowing from a spectrum of conceptual materials and social science disciplines in order to move toward a solution, at a pace suited to the client. The client may be a person, group, organization or whole community.

5

Social Work in Remote Communities

There are few communities, and no societies, left in North America where foragers live untouched by industrial capitalism and its ideology. There are, however, traditional aboriginal groups in the throes of cultural and economic change brought about by outside forces. In these traditional communities the old ways must exist alongside, or in conflict with, the imported system.[1] Traditional ways are under great pressure, and their manifestations may be radically changed by the community's effort to survive. Sometimes traditions are hidden in order to save them from external pressure; sometimes the people develop creative adaptations or they are able to integrate the traditions into their emerging dependent economy. However, the overall hope for the survival of these communities with some kind of economic and cultural independence is slim.

The pattern of cultural and economic breakdown is similar wherever hunting and gathering people live in close proximity to industry and the apparatus of the state: original tongues give way to the language of the schools and legal system; the orally transmitted stories of the people are eclipsed by the stories of the dominant people through magazines, books, radio and television; kinship obligations are eroded by the structures of the nuclear family imported from the city; the old forms of male/female and young/old relationships are subjected to the debates current in the outside society. Traditional political structures give way to the political organization of the state; craft skills are lost; hunting and gathering and early agricultural forms are replaced by welfare, partial wage labour and dependence; money exchange gradually becomes the economic mode; and communities are relocated at the convenience of the state or industry. Corporations pollute, expropriate and exploit the traditional foraging grounds of the people. For each broken social and economic structure there is a victory of sorts for the new way — some call it progress, some call it genocide.[2]

An aboriginal town on the corner of a lake thrived there for over one hundred years. The people made their living by fishing, hunting and trapping. The town stretched along the lake shore, and the local people were familiar with the trap lines, hunting territories and fishing bays, and who used them.

During a period of a few years, large outside corporations began commercial timbering within a few miles of the town, and some local men had taken to cutting trees on a casual basis. The cutting destroyed some trapping and hunting areas. As the timbering grew in area and economic importance, the government made overtures to the people to move the town across the lake, beside a new highway, close to another lake which was thought to be ideal for a tourist development. In time, through various methods of persuasion and community development procedures, the townspeople agreed to the move.

New houses were to be built, largely by the people themselves, with their work counting as "sweat equity." That work, together with employment on the highway, the school, the streets, the sewer and water-systems and the rest, would provide income to make down payments on the housing.

Due to an amazing series of administrative errors, many workers had no deductions taken from their paycheque, and thus found they had no down payments on their houses when the time came to move in. The school was not ready, but to force the people to move, the government closed the school at the old town. Many of the new houses had no furnace hooked up, and the school had only a furnace with no ducts. Fall arrived. It snowed, but the people were prevented from entering their houses unless they could make the down payment. People lived in tents in the front yards of their houses. Children were getting sick. There was no reliable clean water supply. Sewage and garbage lay in soggy, icy pools among the humps of snow. Social workers attempted unsuccessfully to provide down payments through social assistance. The people appealed to government officials to do something about the dreadful living conditions, lack of schooling, and the administrative nightmare in their midst.

Finally, in desperation, aboriginal organization leaders meeting with the responsible official invited him for "lunch" and drove him down the new highway to see this fiasco in person. They told him he could have his lunch when this mess was cleared up. The official was able to order the houses opened, the administrative wheels turned, and the school opened. Over a period of months problems were solved, only as a result of firm interventions by social workers, nurses, and other government officials. The people are now all on salaries, own businesses or are on welfare.

The name of the town, in the local aboriginal language, means "swearing" in English.

Postscript: A news clipping tells us that the wooden basements of those houses were treated with creosote and penta-chlorophenyl (PCP) to prevent rotting. Side-effects are chronic asthma and unnamed "health problems," according to the Canadian Council of Ministers of the Environment. Their publication notes that wood treated with creosote and PCPs should not be used in indoor construction.[3])

In whose interest?

How do social workers fit into this disassembling of a society? Can they adjust their function in order to assist communities to resist such pressures? Some say that social workers cannot work for aboriginal peoples. They declare social work to be a contradiction in terms in that it offers no survival skills which an aboriginal community desperately needs. An astute student once referred to his fellow social workers as "the shock troops of the army of occupation" of remote areas. To continue the military metaphor, we are the mop-up operation and the propaganda machine as well, all at the same time.

The fact that social work is one of the intrusive forces from industrial society into remote areas is rarely recognized in social work textbooks, by lecturers, theorists or area supervisors. The social worker is sent in with a job defined by the agency bureaucracy as one of control and regulation, and by the profession as one of healing social wounds and shoring up "civilization." There is no discussion of whose interests are served when the social worker is sent into a remote community. It must be assumed to be the interests of the employer, to be accomplished in an "objective" and "rational" manner. People should conduct their lives in an orderly, hard-working fashion because this is the way things should be. The world view of the agency may be utterly opposed to that of the community. The agency may, in fact, be actively assisting to destroy that world. But that is the job.

When social work is carried to cultures unconnected to industrialism, all sorts of dislocations occur. The classification systems used in industrial society do not work well in aboriginal cultures; and since social work can carry a certain view of the world, by this very nature it can be disrespectful of other world views. Social workers who attempt to impose these views on aboriginal peoples frequently find that "nothing seems to work." Even if they are well acquainted with the remote culture and have eased tensions between themselves and their clients, social workers still face failure. It is evident that simply being sensitive to the forms and social relations of the aboriginal community is not enough. Social workers must actually refashion the way they do their job. They must reject old ways of ordering information and rethink their assumptions about how society works and how people within it relate to each other and the world. It is one thing to go fishing with your client, but quite another to create new ways which will enable the client to continue to be able to fish. There is a place for a social worker committed to the people of the community, but the place must be built on new alignments, new understandings and an adapting of the duties of the job to basic community organizing principles.

The profession provides little preparation to social workers for work in remote areas with aboriginal peoples. Naturally if social workers venture into foreign situations with little idea of the conditions and issues they will face (carrying a baggage of myths, half-truths and misunderstandings), they will feel threatened when confronted by the realities of the job. If ignorance and fear get the better of them, a sense of despondency and immobility is almost inevitable. After six months of struggling with the job and dealing with people they regard as uncommunicative, distrustful and difficult, many workers long to throw in the towel. If they stay, they become cynical and deskbound in an effort to hold the line against these incomprehensible people and their messy, incoherent lives.

Which side are you on?

Rural social workers, to be effective, must know who they are working for. When the urban population organized itself during the industrial revolution, early social workers in settlement houses, clinics, relief lines and workers' organizations regarded themselves as participants in the struggle. They identified with the poor and the powerless. The social workers committed themselves to the people for whom they were working, and their support was derived partly from within the community itself.

Today, however, even within the dominant culture, helping workers are often from professional family backgrounds while those they treat come largely from the working class, the underclass, the forgotten and set aside. They are most successful with people most like themselves, those who are highly motivated to help regain a stable and respectable place in society. This is not surprising, nor does it diminish the positive help which social work can accomplish with those so motivated.

But where a clash of cultures exists, it is critical that the social worker becomes partisan. Social work services are foreign to the aboriginal community, though the need for these services grows as the fabric of the foraging culture tears and its alternatives for action narrow. Unless social workers can adjust their work among aboriginal organizations to reflect the needs of the community instead of the requirements of the agency, their activities inevitably hurry along the destruction of the culture. After all, in the final analysis, that is what the job is designed to do.

It is difficult to change social work practices to pursue different ends. But the choice of serving only the interests of the employer leads to predictable, often tragic results: authoritarian practice, less and less sympathy with the problems of the community, and increasingly defensive posturing. The social worker who takes this stand is nothing more than a colonial administrator charged with the responsibility of transforming the community into orderly, tidy, dependable working people or, failing that, of assuring that docile, passive observers do not interfere with "progress."

In the interests of the client

During training, the social worker is instilled with a sense of authority and power over the client. The worker in the field knows the regulations and how to employ them. To admit ignorance about the people in the community in which you are working is to have this sense of power and authority threatened. Back in the city, adept use of technique to accomplish ends swiftly is valued, not only for the purpose of doing the job well, but for maintaining and enhancing one's feelings of personal self worth (and, let us not forget, a comfortable income). During the time that the social worker is getting his or her feet wet in the new community, it is difficult to make oneself feel safe and personally supported.

"Sometimes the only way you can cope with the newness of it all is to do the job as prescribed by the agency from nine in the morning till five at night and find your way around the community in your time off," one social worker commented. Another observer noted, "Occasionally a supervisor might bend orthodox practices around the office, to recognize the realities, but it is rare. When this happens, the new social worker can afford the relative luxury of finding out about the people without constantly fighting the agency rulebook. Usually, however, as a worker gains understanding of the problems of the people around him he becomes more and more ambivalent in his job and is forced into clever deceptions, long paper battles and careful maneuvering if he wants to stay."

Social workers should not expect to be automatically awarded a friendly reception simply because they align themselves with the community. Their intentions may be noble, but they remain in the same structural relation to the people as any professional. The skills which they offer the people are drawn from the social worker's industrial society; if the people can use the worker's skills to secure some protection for themselves from the intruding society or to develop a way of living with it, then the workers have begun to put down roots in the community.

In some cases friendships grow between social workers and members of the community, and purely service relationships coexist without threat. Sometimes social workers can live in the area before taking on the agency job and become acquainted with the people before the functional relationship begins. Living in the same community as your clients is important. Living in the same part of the community allows social workers and community members to work together, carry on traditional activities together, share food and drink, and face problems together. The understandings that flow out of these situations occur only when people know each other in day-to-day life. (Indian reserves may be one type of exception, where the functions of the welfare system and functions of the kinship system not only overlap, but power relations imposed by government departments make social and professional interchange mutually exclusive in many cases.)

In a small community in northern Canada there was a local town council and an aboriginal organization which were active, made good decisions, and were solidly in touch with the people. The community had already developed into an agricultural phase, which had grown out of their earlier foraging, but the intrusion of the white man and the fur trade had destroyed it. The town had half-consciously recaptured some of the old ways of living, of doing things and solving problems; it had, in fact, partially returned to hunting and gathering. The social worker was seen as a sort of problem solver, and as my predecessors had been sensitive social workers, I was accepted without fear or hostility.

On a number of occasions, when child care or health

concerns were problems, the first and best resources were the town council and the aboriginal organization. They would quickly, and informally, find a temporary home for a child, or find a ride to the hospital ninety miles away.

I felt welcome socially as well as officially. One fond recollection is the grand opening of the "old folks' home" built by their organization. They shot more than forty ducks and geese, and made bannock, Labrador tea and birch syrup for the festivities. The few white official "outsiders" in the community were the invited guests at the head table.

Obviously, such opportunities to learn about a new environment are not always available, but somehow the social worker must become familiar with the life of the people, thereby building respect for the traditions of that society and acting with integrity as an outsider.

Among traditional aboriginal peoples the young and old have special cultural responsibilities. The old are respected and hold powerful roles in the community; they are integral to the whole community, not just to their immediate families. They are repositories of information and knowledge and pass along the history (and most importantly, the ways of the people) to the young. In a society where myth and history are transferred orally and where there is no question about their relevance to the people, the elders of a society perform a vital function.

The young, especially the children, support the old, bring them hope and joy, take on the ways of the people, and use traditions to honour the old. Supporting the old is not a "legal" obligation, but is required as a practicality, for only the old can pass on to the young the lessons of survival.

The most useful activity for a social worker in such a society is listening. In the consumer society back in the city the ability to absorb things slowly is not highly regarded; old ways are quickly outdated and forgotten and "newness" is rewarded without much thought about what is being pushed aside. But in a remote village if the social worker can be quiet for a moment and if the time and place are right, if one has the trust of the speaker, the worker might be honoured with some of the stories of the people. These stories teach deeply; they bring an understanding far beyond their simplicity.

Contrary to many myths generated for the purpose of industrial society, the natural elements are the friends of hunting and gathering peoples. It is the white man who battles the elements. In the Cree language, "thunder" is the same word as that for "swan." Spoken roughly, forcefully, it means "thunder." A young man told me of the time his grandfather taught him the word, and how to say it. The grandfather did not explain why it was so.

One morning, very early, this young man was out collecting firewood in the muskeg (swamp) with his grandfather. There was a thick mist. The sun was shining through it, making the day warm. Suddenly he heard the beating of big birds' wings close above him. He ducked in fright.

His grandfather said the word.

Swan.

Thunder.

Unlearning

While you are learning, you are also unlearning. Prejudices, misconceptions and falsifications have to be carefully stripped away. Some will be obvious from the beginning, some will succumb to intelligent research and reading, while others crumble under the influence of experience with the people. However, there are deep-seated and popular prejudices which are difficult to undo. They have been knit into the dominant ideology and help to keep racism alive and well. A few of the more insidious are presented here to caution social workers that cultural biases block understanding.

If you fly into a village and find half the adult population out hunting, you might conclude — if you regard the life of these people to be bleak, brutal and poor — that they have to hunt or they will starve to death. If, however, you know the traditions and rituals of the hunt and understand its place in the economy of the village, you might find the emptiness of the village to be a sign of strength. The first assumption might lead you to try to find an entrepreneur to set up a grocery store. The second might lead to creation of an income support strategy so the hunt can continue. Of course, your first assumption might be true; indeed the people might starve to death if they did not shoot game (although the social worker and the people both probably have some alternatives before starvation actually occurs). But you have understood very little if that is all you understand.

Misconception 1: The short, brutal life of the hunter

City people regard the hunting and gathering life as a dirty, hand-to-mouth existence, with starvation lurking just around the corner. But there is evidence that where food and game are abundant, the foraging life is easier than the life of the industrial worker.[4] The notion of a way of life that does not produce surplus is puzzling to members of money economies and class societies. Foraging people do starve at times — this occurred more frequently in North America after contact with Europeans, who through the fur trade forced concentrated population patterns on foraging peoples. Notions of accumulation are so deeply ingrained in European culture that the necessary lack of burdensome belongings among foraging people appears to be a hardship.

Misconception 2: Poverty is the lack of non-essentials

Many aboriginal people in North America are, both by their definition and ours, poor. Many have been made poor by the dire effects of "progress." In these communities certain depressingly universal proofs (so-called "social indicators") of poverty exist and are immediately visible — poor nutrition, extreme health problems, high infant and maternal mortality rates, low life expectancy, high unemployment, high welfare dependence, and shoddy clothing and housing. Closely linked to these conditions of poverty are serious signs of cultural disintegration — alcoholism and other drug use, breakdown of kinship bonds, family violence, child neglect, high suicide rates, and an extreme rise in physical and sexual assault and murder.

It is also true, and less recognized that those communities which continue to make their living from the land and preserve a strong foraging culture might look poor to the outsider but, in fact, are not. In these communities prosperity must be measured by a different yardstick from that used in industrial society. Where a definition of poverty in the consumer society might be "poverty is the lack of non-essentials," in a foraging community it might be "poverty is the lack of essentials."

Instead of getting into a spurious and self-defeating argument about what is and what is not "essential," the social worker would be well advised to consider whether the people see themselves as poor. If the answer is no, the next step is to look around to see what makes the community prosperous. It may be as simple a list as adequate food supply, warm shelter, and possession of the equipment needed for the activities of the hunt — and particularly the relationships that go along with them. If the people are happy, peaceful and healthy, then they prosper, both by their definition and ours. If they do not kill each other, disgrace their elders, drink heavily and die from unnecessary health hazards, then they prosper.

Such communities manifest a strong attachment to the original foraging culture and sturdy resistance to the encroaching industrial culture. The ability of these communities to remain prosperous, however, is not a matter of innate superiority over the next village downriver. Many factors come into play — from the strength of the village chief to how much the uranium cartel wants the land they are living on.

Inadequate definitions of poverty present many problems to the social worker. In North America the "poverty line" is defined by statisticians and social service bureaucrats who apply tests to urban and suburban populations. These same tests are then applied to isolated villages in a remote area. Transplanted to such a remote community, or even to an Indian reserve next to a city, these standards do not make much sense, simply because the wrong data is incorporated into their calculations. In many remote communities the cost of food in a grocery store, for instance, may vary from 50 percent to 500 percent higher than in the city; a trip to the hospital may include a $1000 or more airfare; the presence or absence of food gathered from the bush can determine the quality of nutrition; the wish to purchase imported store food may vary with the season, availability of hunters and government-imposed game regulations. In other words, wealth may not be assessable under imported definitions, and any attempts to apply them can lead the social worker into a minefield of misunderstandings.

A village in northern Canada existed until recently almost entirely outside the money economy. A priest visited there by flying in aboard a float plane and enrolled the elders for the Old Age Security pension and other financial and benefit supplements. Until then all villagers had lived on trapping, fishing, ber-

ries, wild game and other natural provender. Money was almost never in their possession for more than a few minutes, being handled only when they brought their furs into the trader's store where they immediately paid off their debts, or "grubstakes." They then indebted themselves once again, buying nets, traps, bullets, flour, sugar and other basic goods on credit. What little money they might retain was used for a magnificent "beer bust" on the riverbank before travelling upstream again for eight days, hauling their loaded canoes with small motors against the current of the northern rivers. There was no road or street in their village, no stores, no hotel. Just cabins in the winter and tents in the summer.

Money was not needed. Radio and television would be superfluous. They were happy, lived well together and up to that point had no need of the attentions of social workers.

One's assumption here might have been that people need a constant supply of food available in the marketplace to remain healthy. It is difficult to grasp that people might wish to continue what urban dwellers view as the feast-or-famine luck of the hunt. It might help to know, then, that physical anthropologists have determined that pre-contact First Nations people were healthier than those of the present day and had as long a lifespan as Laplanders (in the north of Finland), who still live much like North American aboriginal peoples used to. Hamburger, sugar, "enriched" bread, and noodles do not contribute much to health.

When the pensions first started arriving, they sat in the post office for months until the villagers came with their furs. The oldsters found they could not possibly spend it all on beer, and they didn't like the cafe food or store groceries. They declined to buy hard items because there was not enough room in the canoes to carry them all back upriver.

Instead they spent the money on bigger boat motors, motor toboggans and other machines which were driven back upriver after freezeup in the fall. They soon discovered that machines need repairs, new parts, gas and oil. Then they needed bigger boats and bigger motors to haul their supplies back to the village. More gas, more oil, more repairs. Some began chartering airplanes on floats to carry the bigger loads and make the trips faster. More money needed.

As a new social worker, I accepted their applications, from which the government offices in the south could ascertain how much pension they were "eligible" for. The application forms, designed for the city, were difficult to complete. "How much do you spend on gas?" actually referred to natural gas, for cooking or heating. The villagers used wood for such purposes, so we wrote down an appropriate figure per year for gas for the boats and the motor toboggans. "What are your transportation costs?" it would ask. The manual told us that this referred to bus fare used to go downtown and shop or go to the doctor. They would answer that it cost twelve days of gas, oil and food to go shopping downriver in the nearest town.

It was fun filling out those silly forms, and we would laugh uproariously together. They would ask me what it was like to live in those big towns like Vancouver anyway. Then, a few weeks later, the money would come, and they would pick up their cheques, buying nylon parkas that would wear out in a week in the bush, or blue jeans whose seams were already unravelling before they got out of the store. They might have had more money, but they were getting poorer. The real recipients of the new income were the merchants in town.

The social worker will be forced to construct an entirely new understanding of the economic health of the community in which he or she works. While it is clear that a city whose workers have been thrown out of jobs by plant closure is getting poorer, it is not as clear when a remote community starts to go downhill, poised as it is betwixt subsistence on the land, part-time wages, government assistance and resource exploitation. As usual the social worker has to look to the people for information — there is no one who knows any better.

Misconception 3: Crazy means crazy anywhere

It should be no surprise to anyone that societies as different in their economies and cultures as foraging societies are from industrial societies are also dramatically different in their psychologies. Social workers' practices, increasingly focused on the personal and psychological aspects of society (if governments and private agencies get their way) and less and less on the social and political aspects, are especially adept at distorting, misreading and abusing the psychology of aboriginal peoples. Many outsiders who learn to read the "objective" facts of hunting and gathering economies, even to the point of adapting the laws and regulations involved in their jobs, find it difficult to respect the "subjective" fact that aboriginal peoples do not share the same world view as they do.[5]

When a society is under attack, so is its entire view of the world. As the society breaks down, its members start to break down as well. This happens at all levels. Thus comprehensive understanding — economic, social, religious and psychological — of the people's world view is vital for a social worker, who characteristically deals more frequently with individual and family problems than with problems pertaining to the social and economic health of the community.

The patterns of emotional and mental distress among

aboriginal peoples which we all see (and which the media love to exploit) are repeated time and again in community after community as each comes under obvious pressure to assimilate. Characteristic responses to cultural breakdown are alcoholism, soaring suicide rates, high rates of imprisonment, child neglect, beatings, murder and other violence in the home and community. These responses are not unique to aboriginal populations and occur with cultural variations in many societies whose economic and cultural base is being destroyed. The process continues until the people either die or are assimilated, unless there is a strong, politically adept, culturally viable resistance.

Many social workers new to aboriginal villages encounter these problems immediately and quickly reduce them to "mental illness," a sort of mass sickness which is consuming the local society. The medical model has certainly proved a very handy method for explaining our world; among other things, it allows us to ignore the social and political causes of capitalism's defects. To conclude that someone is sick, whether as a result of a microbe or mental imbalance, implies that we do not have to look further than the individual for a cure. Yet it becomes obvious that treatment of social breakdown with individualistic psychological techniques is both inadequate and short sighted. This is so even in an industrialized society. It is even more so among people whose social structure differs from ours and who do not share our assumptions about why people fall ill or act crazy.[6]

No one would deny that a society with high rates of violence, suicide, depression and alcoholism is in trouble. But the most common mistake is to see that society as the source of its own trouble — to "blame the victim."[7] It is difficult not to: if you enter an aboriginal community without an understanding of the people's history, and of how they have been affected by it, it is almost inevitable that you will blame them for their troubles. Popular neo-conservative theories which glorify the role of free will and individual choice predispose many social workers to assign blame to their clients. And this blame tends to find its way into treatment. In other words, you see a family that has an alcoholic mother and a drunken, violent father and two children who have been beaten. You decide that the solution is to provide therapy, place the children in a stable foster home, put the mother in a good alcoholism program and find the father a job. None of these interventions are intrinsically evil; but why is it, year after year, none seem to be working? Briefly, the success of any action requires that one's efforts be tied to the traditional life of the community and generated by the community itself. All programs must exist within economic or emotional support structures provided by the community. Misunderstanding and then bypassing the community undermines the possibility of providing effective help.

Every society has its own explanation for illness. Every society has healers and its own way of reintegrating the disturbed or diseased person. These understandings emerge from a world view, that is, from the way that a people look out on and explain the world. These explanations satisfy; they do not require further questioning — that, simply, is the way things are. They are real and true as far as the individuals are concerned, whether in an industrial society or in a hunting and gathering society. Simply put, the difference between the way that aboriginal societies and industrial societies explain disease is that for the latter, disease is the result of infection, pathology and bodily malfunction, while for the former it is the result of transgression, immorality and witchcraft. Each view has its own justifications and carries its own sanctions. Each view is ministered to by its own healers and rituals. Obviously if the person you are trying to heal abides by, and believes in, the principles of another world view, you are going to have trouble with your healing.

Traditional aboriginal medicine continues today, just as traditional ways of looking at the world and the traditional economies continue to exist in varying degrees. Traditional healing continues to function whether or not the social worker, surrounded by the apparatus of healing available in his or her culture, accepts its presence. Social workers do not have to become expert in this form of healing, but they must recognize it as a fact, respect it and abide by the social rules that accompany it.

North American aboriginal societies view illness as an individual transgression against the social order or the spirit world, a violation of a taboo or the result of another's bad medicine against the patient. Serious illnesses have moral implications; they are "associated with some prior conduct which involved an infraction of moral rules ... a penalty for bad conduct."[8] To get better is not so much a matter of healing the body, but of healing the wound in society. In traditional society, disease is seen as a violation of a moral rule, a tension which has to be resolved before the community is free from threat. The distinction which industrial society makes between mental and physical illness is not particularly instructive in this system — if a man in aboriginal society "goes crazy" or if he has an attack of gallstones, its source is the same, and the need for the village to discern the cause and for the patient to set things straight is the same.

Among aboriginal societies, exerting social control is paramount. Behaviour is not easily altered, because the land and the spirits have provided a living to the people when they used behaviour that has always worked in the past. Odd behaviour and illness represent the need to correct the patient's relationship with the spirits and the land, to organize behaviour along proven lines. It is damaging for an outside agent like a social worker to disrupt the beliefs and practices of healing; to do so would erode what the hunters and gatherers know to be true from their own experience.

Of course, the aboriginal population of North America is largely no longer able to pursue hunting and gathering. After three hundred years of contact with industrial society, foraging life has changed drastically. Some traditional forms remain strong, some forms have disappeared entirely; many exist only in part. In most aboriginal communities Indian medicine and medicine of the industrial society exist in close proximity, and the people use both. Aboriginal healers are sometimes even covered by government insurance plans to treat illnesses which do not respond to orthodox medicine. At times, sufferers see their illnesses as being of two types — aboriginal and white man's — and the proper medicines are applied accordingly.

Although some psychiatrists and psychologists have recognized the importance of social factors and family in the development of some mental disorders, the field remains dominated by medical explanations. While these explanations do not enter directly into the counselling which a social worker engages in, they form a backdrop for his or her understandings. In addition Freudian analysis, with its emphasis on childhood traumas and levels of consciousness, can provide certain insights. But without reworking the treatment system entirely, both Western medicine and Freudian theory simply become more nails in the coffin for the aboriginal culture.

In the final analysis psychological treatment is not so much a cultural question as it is a political one. Industrial societies have, through their governments, decided what range of behaviour is acceptable. This range is much narrower than that tolerated in foraging or agricultural societies. The industrial society uses its powers to penetrate the regions occupied by hunting and gathering and agricultural peoples, and the use of mental health ideas and treatments are ways of enforcing codes of behaviour necessary for the functioning of the industrial economy, even at its periphery. The most sensitive social worker can try to blunt the damage caused by Western medicine on hunting and gathering people, but if there is no political understanding of how industrial medicine and psychology work as agents of assimilation, then any efforts can meet with only limited success.

A 15-year-old girl from a northern community in Canada was known to be selling sex so she would not have to stay at home. Her parents drank; some of the other children had been taken into foster care. Her behaviour was seen as an emotional disturbance for some reason, and she was taken into care and placed in a centre for treatment in a large southern city.

There she learned about taking drugs, stealing and forgery, and acquired a certain expertise in car theft. At the same time, she began an intense correspondence with a northern social worker about how her family was doing — the family she had always tried to flee.

As the correspondence developed, the social worker learned about the efforts which had been made to get the family to leave the trap line, to enter salaried, seasonal work, to get the children to attend school, and about the rapid slide into alcoholism, family violence and the rest. The family resisted and fought against leaving the life they knew and wanted. During a few short years, all the families in that town left trapping, drank, beat up on each other and lost, at least temporarily, the struggle against being bound to the town and to money.

The young woman's father and mother and the youngest of the children finally escaped back to trapping and the bush, along with some others who just wanted to escape from the violence, alcohol and disruptive life of the town. The young woman was thrilled for them, happy that they would be happy. But for her there was no way to join them, not only because she was being held for treatment in the city, but because she did not know the trapping life, had no bush skills, and would only be a hindrance to them. She knew that.

In her letters she said that after leaving the institu-

tion she would go to Vancouver or Toronto and live there. Once she made it to the big city, she drifted eas-ily into the peripheral world of petty crime and the city sex trade, and stopped writing. She knew the social worker would be disappointed in her.[9]

And another kind of story.

An acquaintance of the author tells of a family she worked with as a social worker and counsellor. The wife was in a mental institution in a large city, hundreds of miles away from her husband and children. She said her husband was practising bad medicine on her. Cer-tainly he was beating her and the children when she was at home, and there was incest as well. One child suffered from cerebral palsy and was mentally handi-capped. The children were eventually placed in foster homes in the same city as the mother.

Through family counselling sessions the social worker aimed to reunite the family at their home on the Indian reserve. However, she simply could not get them even to talk to each other. The woman, alone, would say she wanted to get well. The husband, alone, would say he was miserable inside. They both said they wanted to look after their children, but the com-munication between the parents was nil. The man's bad medicine made it impossible for husband and wife to do anything together; at one point, hoping to get them talking about anything, the social worker cried out to the man and woman, "Don't you want your kids? Because if you want them, you just have to try and work and fight for them!"

Nothing. There was no response. She was not even close to their world. It was not her fault; she had noth-ing to offer them except the institutions and the treat-

ment methods and the control mechanisms of the white man's world. They didn't know what to do with these things, and they could only hold them off by silence.

In the cities of North America a large number of aboriginal organizations are being built which offer help — treatment if you like. The members of these organizations know the effect of bad medicine, of the spirits, of the revenge the land and elements can take if they are abused. The organizations are starting up schools in which their people can learn how to cope. Many are called "survival schools." The name is instructive, for it tells us what the stakes are for them. Most rural areas do not have these institutions; there the remaining fragments of the old ways of surviving still provide shelter for those unable to cope. Social workers need to become familiar with both the new and the old organizations, and need to learn how to make use of them.

The new procedures do not mean abandonment of regular social work. They may mean the creation of parallel activities which the people can control themselves and from which the social worker can learn.

Languages carry many assumptions of which their speakers are hardly aware, and outsiders often violate these assumptions, being ignorant of how the culture and the language support each other. Foragers' languages virtually never use the "either-or" construction of European tongues. The forager's vocabulary is heavily weighted toward process words, made up of word cores, prefixes and suffixes that tell what is happening, how, where, etc., rather than trying to present ideas as still pictures — slices of life cut out of time, as it were. In dealing with foragers, therefore, social workers should know that a question like "Are you working or not!" is not, strictly speaking, a valid question. Hunting people rarely distinguish between work, leisure, learning, or other aspects of life. Life is an encompassing process, in which there is neither a separation between doing one thing and doing another, nor between one person doing it and another person doing that same thing.

Likewise, due to the place of the individual in the collective life of the people, many notions like guilt, motivation, thoughts ascribed to others, and many other constructions peculiar to the languages of industrial people just do not appear in hunters' languages.

6

Social Work in Rural Agricultural Societies

Almost all agriculture in North America takes place within the structures of the marketplace. While non-market and subsistence agriculture are rarities on the continent, it is worthwhile to examine the transition from foraging to agriculture.

The transition of societies from the foraging stage was related to the discovery that animals and plants could be domesticated (or, perhaps more accurately, this discovery was forced on them by external pressures of geography, powerful enemies or natural disaster). The demise of foraging economies marked the onset of a non-market stage of agriculture. While farmers traded produce sporadically when they had a surplus, there were no regular systems of sale or exchange, the bulk of crops and animal products being consumed by those growing them.

In the early stages — before advanced growing practices, irrigation, fertilizing, storage and the like were practised — this form of agriculture could further be described as subsistence agriculture. On the whole there was no surplus, and grown products often were supplemented by foraged goods.[1]

During this stage the manner in which people related to each other began to change dramatically. Individuals and their families began to acquire animals, plots of land and buildings. As early agriculture evolved over thousands of years, the responsibility for property gradually changed into ownership of that property. The extended family as a means of tending that property and passing it from one generation to another had its roots in this economic phase.

The owners assumed powers which we recognize today, through which they gained land tenure, animal ownership, storage capacity for seed and surplus, and the like. In other words they began to amass capital. Individuals took personal credit for production. This bolstered their arguments for increased rights over land and animals to enhance production even further. As well, it was a means of gaining control of more of the resources needed for agriculture, and a means of accumulating the best animals, land, seed, etc., to further secure their position.

Protection and expansion of these holdings frequently required the use of force. The warriors, who in foraging times fought only when threatened by other peoples or when additional land was needed, now became a permanent group within the society. They now waged war to amass further capital through plunder and the capture of slaves and animals. Evolution from subsistence agriculture to primitive industrialism involved development of ever-larger landholdings, private armies, and a peasantry reduced to selling its labour after being deprived of its small landholdings. These changes occurred in all parts of the globe at varying times. New technologies and shortages of land provided the impetus. North America and, more recently, some Third World countries have bypassed the feudal stage of agriculture, due to a central industrial economy using an imposed agriculture as a supply source.[2] The older, non-market agricultural economy still exists in some remaining Third World countries.

In North America and Europe the transformation to market agriculture has been completed, not only to ever-higher zeniths of productivity, but also to the ever-increasing attachment of agriculture as a peripheral function of the industrial state. Agriculture itself becomes industrialized. And now, growing farm products depends more and more on petrochemical products sprayed on the plants, injected into the animals, plowed into the earth and applied to the products brought into the stores to make them look nicer and last longer. In recent decades, "Big Pharma Chem" turned its research efforts to capturing licences, trademarks, copyright and other forms of intellectual property right in order to own, sell, or otherwise distribute genetically modified organisms (GMOs). These take the form of altered seeds, combined chromosomes, cloned animals, fish or birds and so forth. Big agricultural companies sell them to farmers and ranchers, as well as to fishers and hunters, on contract bases that guarantee the big petrochemical and drug companies a profit on every organism grown, sold, transported or offered for research. Legal court cases launched by the big pharmaceutical companies now seem aimed at controlling all aspects of food production and sales on the globe.

Advanced market agriculture inhabits almost all the food-source land in North America. Hunting and foraging as well as subsistence or non-market agriculture have almost disappeared, the few exceptions being minuscule social experiments in North America, Britain and elsewhere in which members engage in ideologically motivated communal farm projects. Though these are not options for the vast majority of farm families, they could serve as useful sources of information. Most of these utopian efforts have resulted only in failed dreams and/or financial disaster for participants.[3] The only other examples are in remote areas where market agriculture has not yet penetrated.

Market agriculture assumes a variety of forms and these are reflected in related patterns of social organization. A social worker, in order to intervene effectively, needs an understanding of both the type and formation of market agriculture in which the clients are engaged and the resulting social patterns.

In North America there are still farmers who regularly sell only a small part of their produce, using the rest themselves. On some farms the land is worked by several generations of the same family. These extended farm families, though a rarity, represent one end of the spectrum of social forms seen in North American agriculture. Parents, children, grandparents and occasionally other blood relations live and work together, often sharing a single farmhouse, sometimes occupying a cluster of houses, but all using a common landholding. Frequently these families are able to produce a wide variety of farm goods, from poultry and cattle to vegetables, cereal crops and fruits. The spread of age and ability levels offers a wide scope for varying kinds of work, energy and time commitment.

At the other extreme are farms run as virtual industrial "land business" enterprises, often producing only one crop or animal for market purposes alone. No part of the product is consumed by those who work the landholding. The latter are hired on a salary or wage basis. No family formation is found there, unless an employee happens to have brought a spouse and children, if housing had been available. It is not unusual for workers to be seasonally employed, leaving the farmholding for other work when the growing season is over. In rare cases farmworkers employed by an agricultural company with holdings in a variety of locations might move from one to the other for seeding, harvesting, repair work and the like as the seasons progress. Sometimes workers are brought from the city by bus for daily work.

Between these extremes is what is thought of as the typical North American farm, the family farm, run as a family enterprise with adults working the land and raising their children. Some family farms fall into the subsistence category in which products are grown largely for home use, with only a small portion left for marketing. Others operate like the semi-industrial enterprises of the agricultural corporation, but are run by a family, with hired hands being employed for parts of the growing season.

Each of these modern North American farm types presents to the social worker particular kinds of social formations. Some social formations, such as the nuclear farm family or extended farm family, having in most cases firm networks of resources, tend not to present problems for which social work is seen as a remedy. Others, like those groupings of people found in the agribusiness enterprise, often do not make use of social work services. Interruptions caused by migration, tolerance of eccentric or pathological behaviour in the farmworkers' community, and the illegal status of the workers who lack proper immigration papers, partly account for the gulf between these farmworkers and social workers. Social work in rural North America tends to be directed to more "typical" farmers who are members of nuclear families, but who do not have good social resource networks. Such families live in one location long enough to be able to take advantage of services. Yet even here barriers exist which have their roots in the earlier, non-market stage of agriculture. These patterns of behaviour, responsibility and sanction for the giving and receiving of help affect the performance of social work.

Feudalism was the culmination of European nonmarket agriculture. It was also the period of time that witnessed the transformation into market agriculture and laid the foundation of industrial society. The most successful of the prefeudal agriculturists grabbed the powers available to them in this time of great social transformation and established themselves as the landed nobility. Economic and social forces imposed responsibility upon the new aristocracy for those peasants working their holdings. While the peasantry might be subject to their feudal lord, they also held certain expectations of their masters. The nobleman supervised farming and also secured his subjects from danger, attack, starvation and other disasters. As agriculture progressed toward the modern farm, these mutually recognized powers and responsibilities evolved but did not disappear. Many farm families still hold to beliefs that the head of the farm, usually the man, has powers over his family and responsibilities which are not shared by any outside agent, for instance, a social worker. These beliefs and attitudes reflect practical patterns that allowed farm life to produce goods in an earlier era. They do not reflect the fact that the resources to act on these beliefs are often no longer present. When an outside agent tries to bring new types of resources to bear on rural social problems, the farm population is slow to adapt its beliefs and practices to accept the innovations. In fact there are often still practical reasons for rejecting types of help not sanctioned by the rural economic and social system.

Reinforcing this response to outside help or interference is the fact that in frontier North America, farms operated independently; farms were productive units sufficient unto themselves. They had to operate that way. Historical, economic and social forces gave rise to conditions whereby the modern farmer may still view himself as head of a "fiefdom," with those living and working on his land remaining his responsibility. This interpretation of his status, usually shared by relatives and neighbours, makes it difficult for a farm head or family member to accept help or criticism, even when it may be needed.

Historically, the one sanctioned source of help in rural North America was the church. Organized religion originated in Europe and many of the roles of the church stayed the same. It had ties to agricultural life as no other institution had. Aside from the capacity to present an organized helping force throughout almost all rural areas, the church, invested with authority by the state and by local tradition, could carry out helping functions without stigma being attached to the recipient of assistance.[4]

Coupled with these functions were other sources of legitimacy. As the centre of social activity, of legitimation (baptism, marriages and burials) and of education (the church ran the school systems in most parts of North America, the last of which still exist in less developed regions), the church was believed in. This faith had a basis in everyday practice and work. As the frontier closed, as agriculture passed from a subsistence to a market type, as industrialism impinged on farming, and as the resultant social casualties grew in number and force, the church's capacity to continue this helping role stretched to the breaking point. Volume outstripped resources. The government was forced to intervene, initially as the provider of assistance to churches and eventually as the agency that assumed many of the helping functions, especially in the area of charities and other financial assistance.

As government service programs infiltrated rural areas, programs offered were, not surprisingly, modelled on those of the cities. The Great Depression of the 1930s forced government action, especially in the cities. Action in rural areas followed shortly thereafter, funded usually on much the same basis as city services, following the same policies and regulations and hiring the same kinds of people.

The Roosevelt New Deal spelled the end to much of the ongoing discussion about the merits of unique social work practice in rural areas. Josephine Brown was appointed to a key position in the U.S. federal bureaucracy that became the Department of Health, Education and Welfare, ensuring that the urban method of social work would be adopted for rural application. Brown, a partisan in the professional debate,[5] had argued for a unitary social work, to be applied across the United States. Her influence over funding programs and the framing of regulations killed, for official purposes, any recognition of different needs in rural areas.[6] Those arguing for a specific, rural type of social work waned in influence, though they produced a voluminous literature.[7] Canada and much of the industrialized world followed suit.

Social workers in urban and rural areas generally engage in the same activities — public assistance, child and family welfare, corrections, mental health services and counselling. The main difference is that rural areas typically do not have the same level of funding, staffing and, therefore, access to social work as do the cities. Mental health services, especially in the midwestern United States, appear to be the only exception.

In the process of extending programs to rural regions, the effectiveness of urban social work patterns in rural areas again came under question. Evidence of the disadvantages of urban practice in the countryside led to the widely held view that generalist social work practice must replace the classical forms used in the profession. The specialties of "casework, group work and community development," which comprise the foundation of orthodox social work, are detrimental, carrying with them the old forms of colonialism. Accumulated evidence convincingly demonstrates that specialist social work is poorly suited to rural people. Although there may be resistance to reorganizing helping skills into generalist practice, it is a necessary task, one that ought to be undertaken with speed and commitment.

Personal services to individuals

The isolation and independent spirit of traditional rural life does not lend itself easily to asking for, or accepting, help. Social workers often meet with a bleak response or hostility when approaching farmers to inquire about breaking marriages, financial problems, child difficulties or the like. Denial of problems is common, even when the problems are obvious. Just as one must become familiar with the patterns of aboriginal life, and respectful of them, so must the rural social worker become familiar with, and respectful of, farm life. Although city people may share a basic culture with farmsteaders, urban people ("city slickers") do not gain their trust easily.

In order to gain that trust, one large step is to become a part of rural life, even to the extent of doing agricultural work from time to time. It is one thing to study rural farm life, but another to learn through experience what it means to seed, raise poultry, deliver grain to the terminal or salvage grain hit by hail. The farmer is familiar with animal and grain prices, knows when apples need picking and how to sort tomatoes. He follows world market trends in beef. Supplies and schedules, transport and fuel prices and the dangers of pesticides all form a part of the daily life of a farmer. In fact a farmer is a generalist of another sort who assumes of social workers at least a passing acquaintance with the variety of elements of daily farm production. Nothing arouses suspicion more than a social worker bearing help and advice who does not know the nature of the pressures on a farmer.

Of course, it is not possible to list all the items that make up rural life. The nature of the local area, its crops, marketing practices, methods of transport, and the weather and geography, to name only a few, will rule the nature of agricultural practice. Social workers merely need to immerse themselves in Saturday afternoon shopping at the hardware or farm service centre, get to know the grain buyer, follow what people talk about over coffee, and the structure of rural life will begin to emerge.

There is another side to this argument. To be seen as insular and seen as intent on avoiding contact with the world of the farmer is an irreparable mistake. If social workers or the professional community in general seems to be forming a clique that socializes only among themselves, then distance from the local people is all that will be gained. A farmer opposed to revealing problems to an outsider who is obviously a social worker will be more comfortable with someone who is part of the community and can be consulted without displaying to the rest of the community that he or she is asking for or receiving help. And the farmer will be more likely to trust a social worker able to resolve some of the practical problems of farming along with the social ones.

A friend in social work commented often that "social workers in rural areas should be encouraged to learn a useful trade."[8] The ability to weld, shear sheep, pluck chickens, bake bread, change a transmission or fix a pump will be especially helpful in earning credentials in rural areas. Also, knowledge of fieldworkers' unions or rural women's groups and how to organize them can greatly aid the social worker in dealing with rural wage workers on corporate farms or the problems of isolation experienced by many farm women.

While agricultural and urban people share many values and assumptions — such as the worth of the individual, the value of personal responsibility and personal credit for success — many rural people reject the idea that there may be casualties of agriculture. The notion of self-sufficiency on the family farm does not allow for the idea that agriculture itself has potential for damaging people. As agriculture is relentlessly drawn into the periphery of industrial society, rural people sometimes resist the amenities (like modern suburban housing, a second car, the Internet) because these amenities appear to be an admission of a failing ability to cope and be self-sufficient. Farmers, until the recent past at least, knew that money and effort must go first to productive capacity and only later, after producing a surplus, would they purchase luxuries to ease living conditions. But depending on the extent to which a farm participates in the industrial system, "modernization" may run counter to the most deeply held values of the farmsteaders. While buying a computer-assisted tractor, seeder and sprayer is acceptable (since this is a tool), using money for frills and style alone may be seen as a waste. This notion is complicated by trends in finance. Some farms purchase on credit, and even if this drives the residents deep into debt, this often acts to prevent foreclosure, since the bank has invested so much into the farm or ranch already. In the end, though the banks and credit unions do not want to take over and run the farms themselves, the financial institutions know that the land will almost certainly retain enough commercial value to cover loans — even those loans that appear to be somewhat on the frivolous side. So extravagant vehicles and

farm equipment, expensive suburban houses and other purchases that would have been unusual through most of the
20th century are now increasingly common.

Recent cyclical crises in agriculture, caused in part by
slumping world commodity prices, transport competition,
so-called "free trade" agreements and efforts to undermine
government intervention in agriculture through the General Agreement on Tariffs and Trade (GATT) and its succes-
sor organizations like the World Trade Organization, have
begun to convince many farmers that their way of life is
under threat.

In current mythology agriculture still has the aura of rural
scenes in classical paintings in which pastoral farms, the
countryside, clean fresh air, hard work and honesty comprise the rural way of life. There is little perception by farmers of the negative side of rural life. Further, many farmers
regard rural life as offering intangible dividends that offset
any hardship, overcome shortages of the material goods of
the city, and make social and other services a redundancy of
a city culture from which rural people have been spared. It
is therefore difficult for agricultural people to accept social
work and other services as an integral part of their society.
It is almost an admission of faults that rural people hate to
acknowledge.

Urban society, on the other hand, readily admits these
faults and takes credit for handling problems it cannot
avoid. The Great Plains Staff Training and Development for
Rural Mental Health project published a package of materials for rural helping professionals in 1989 to try to address
the unique problems of rural families having trouble holding onto their farms, or who had already been pushed off the
land. *Human Services in the Rural Transition* is a manual
and a videotape (available from the project at the University
of Nebraska-Lincoln), produced with an advisory committee
from Iowa, Kansas, Missouri and Nebraska. A realistic farm
couple talk over the process of confronting the economic

squeeze, the denial, fear, anger, conflict and eventual resolution of their own troubles. In addition, they illustrate how their community can become a resource, a support system and a milieu within which the problems of farm life can be met head on, once those involved admit and share their problems and solutions.

The social worker entering this rural social and economic milieu should not expect a warm welcome. Instead he or she can expect the sour recognition accorded someone who has uncovered an unpleasantness best left under a stone. The skills required to unearth problems and to progress from countering resistance to active problem solving will be available only to the social worker who relates to agricultural people in the same ways as they relate to each other.

A clue to giving and taking help is found in the cooperative movements that grew up among farm producers in many parts of the world. Farm producers, in spite of their independence in some spheres, accept interdependence in areas relating to the production of goods and the maintenance of the production process. Co-operatives, run according to strictly outlined rules, evolved as a unique rural answer to needs for economic interdependence. The important principle in the co-operative movement among farmers is that, in exchange for getting help, each member must be willing to give help as well. No obligation extends beyond the terms established by the co-operative. Personal integrity is maintained. The individual, joined with others who produce the same product and face the same conditions, can beat problems that, alone, would be unsolvable. Yet no charity is involved. Even activities like barn raisings and harvest "bees" are seen as help given in a time of need or disaster, not as a matter of helping the weak or the lazy. It is fully expected that the receiver return the help under similar circumstances. Help offered in the community is given by peers and community members, not by outside experts.

The difference between social workers among North

American farmers and among aboriginal people is that in the former instance they are usually working with their own people. They are not intruders from a colonizing economy penetrating an economic system totally dissimilar from their industrial source. The agricultural person shares with urban people assumptions about work, progress, society and ideology. The social worker can more easily become acquainted with farm production and social relations. Convergence of social worker and farmer in their shared culture is possible then.

Working with farm families

North American farm communities normally are made up of individual families on individual tracts of land. Property ownership is intrinsic to production, and land is passed from one generation to the next. This is a departure from the hunting and gathering phase, during which land was held in common and bands of hunting peoples used the land as nomads, moving with the game and the seasons. In some parts of the world the change from hunting and gathering to agriculture took place over many generations, and the social transformation had time to become established through extended practice, dispute and refinement.

In North America the change was accomplished by imposition, and there was an abrupt break between use of land for foraging and for agriculture. European settlement, for the most part, brought private family ownership of property to rural life, and the methods of passing property from father to son were brought along with the new agricultural base. Farm people still largely see father-headed families as the legitimate form of the social unit. In order for agriculture to work well, not only land but skills must be passed on, and the organization of society into patriarchal families provided a workable formula for bestowing property and skills to use that property. These patterns, enshrined in custom and law, support to this day many of the suppositions about who may inherit property, how it shall be done, and who has the right to decide what is to be done on the farm.

Knowledge of the origins of the agricultural family and the economic reasons for its existence is of great value to a rural social worker.[9] The historical forces which formed the farm family are complex and the social worker needs to know a great deal about them in order to make any kind of intervention. One needs to appreciate the forces at work in the stable family, and to know which are at risk in the family threatened by disintegration.[10]

Industrial society — the overwhelming economic force in North America — has the power to dictate patterns in rural areas. The industrial centres define the modern education system, which many rural people believe entices the young from the farm. Industrial financial institutions increasingly fund agricultural enterprises and remodel them to resemble factory production units. The rural family itself is affected by tax law and by definitions of employment and mobility designed for the purposes of urban industrial society. Of course, rural families are aware of the threat to their continued existence by modern interventions. The property that formed the patriarchal family is now being used in ways which destroy the family.

Social workers have a role in these trends. Since the social worker is an agent of change directed by the needs of industrial society, his or her activities in rural areas often have the appearance, if not the fact, of being a force for change in the interests of the urban culture and economy. Development can be a positive thing, difficult to criticize, yet when applied to rural areas, it often has the effect of rendering the rural regions peripheral to the functions of the dominant industrial society.

Large dairy corporations have been able to control the market in milk in many parts of North America, nar-

rowing the options of farmers considerably. Through the establishment of virtual monopolies in the dairy industry, farmers often may deliver only to one company, have milk transported by it, order containers from it, and have milk prices administered by that same company. Any farmer opposed to the arrangement has no choice but to leave the dairy business or relocate. Recent events in dairy practice requiring standardized methods of handling milk and byproducts which can be financed only by large operators, and which require extra help on the farm beyond what the family can supply, have forced many farmers out of the business.

This example is not an isolated occurrence. Giant land purchases, integration of agricultural production and transport into a single conglomerate, and restrictive laws in farm financing often force farmers to change the way they carry out their activities or to quit.[10]

The social worker is often the agent called in to repair the social damage caused in the course of these changes.

Aside from being responsible for the resolution of problems caused by outside economic forces on the farm, and thus becoming associated with the intrusion, social workers, and other professionals, deliver programs that become part of the intrusion.

Most government-generated rural support programs follow the same model: extend some city amenities into the countryside on the assumption that what city people have, country people should have, too. Social services fall among these amenities. Bring health, counselling, work with young people and similar services to help mend the fabric of rural life, and the increased quality of rural life will encourage families to remain

on their farms. The option to stay in rural areas, rather
than being driven into the city to improve one's quality
of life, is enhanced.
  Or so the thinking goes.

One effect of such developments in rural services is that
they bring salaried people with relatively higher academic
backgrounds and with urban consumption habits and tastes
into the midst of the rural population. Often this leads to
higher prices for housing as better-off people seek accommodation; higher food and leisure costs, for the same reasons;
and often new influences on town, county or municipal
governments that hasten the construction of urban services
like running water, sewerage and paving, which result in
higher taxes. Rural people are often inhibited from opposing such services, yet they rarely initiate such innovations.
Their willingness to accept the programs reflects the (urban)
attitude that surely nobody could be against these things.
Surely the benefits are obvious.

What is not obvious is the cost.

In recent times, tourism has been proposed as a way of
bolstering the rural economy. An unfortunate by-product of
that option is the fact that tourism is almost always highly
seasonal and has the following results: part-time, seasonal
and usually low-paid work, with very few social benefits
such as pension, employment insurance or workers' com-
pensation; the invasion of large numbers of urban people and
their vehicles, creating pressures on local facilities; and the
building of local facilities that have to be paid for even when
the tourists have gone home.

Other urban influences can be recognized. Endorsing farm
mechanization is almost a corollary of industrial influence
on agriculture. Lightening the load of farm work seems sensible and desirable, and nobody, urban or rural, opposes that.
However, mechanization affects not only the labour force,
but the family structure itself.

In its heyday a large farm depended on a relatively large family. The extended family had sufficient labour power to handle all necessary functions. However, mechanization of farm duties reduces the number of people needed. Development in rural areas presses people into mechanization from all sides. The continuity and social organization implicit in labour-intensive farming is lost in a cultural surrounding that emphasizes luxury, comfort and leisure. When efficiency becomes the main consideration, human and animal labour cannot compete. Under these circumstances the family farm comes to mean a nuclear family employing machines on an agricultural holding that must be run increasingly like an industry. When that point is reached, support for family farming of any sort is weakened. A large-scale farm using only seasonal labour begins to make far more sense than a family reliant on its own labour (with the family obliged to support its members throughout the year). Traditional farming families survive only because they have been willing to set aside efficiency as the main consideration and recognize other values, for example, continuity, quality of life, sense of community and the like. These other values almost always mean lower income.

In comparison, we could note two examples of alternative ways of organizing agriculture, two places where an alternative choice was possible. China and Tanzania, because of their non-industrial bases, chose to emphasize and build on agricultural foundations to shape industry rather than the other way around. They are at stages in their economic and cultural life in which moving from foraging to agriculture to industry are all going on to varying degrees and speeds in different parts of their countries.

China's development of communes is based on existing kinship and family patterns. As commune mem-

bers work together, they identify ways in which their work can be lightened through mechanization, and the industrial base begins to grow, founded on a logic plain to all involved.[11] *The need for equipment, fertilizers or a good transport system grows from their daily activity. Recent moves to dismantle the communes of China apparently threaten this pattern, but some citizens defend the gains made by collectivization. William Hinton's books* Fanshen *and* Shenfan *(Monthly Review Press) detail the struggles to collectivize, then privatize, and now to defend the communes.*

*In Tanzania the government based its agricultural policy on a concept called "Ujamaa" or "Familihood." Social workers, educators and organizers indigenous to the local area work together to provide support and encouragement for agricultural life. Farming becomes the base on which inducements are made for people to remain in the rural areas and for locally based industry to grow.[12] However, their approach has been criticized for many things, not the least of which is its failure to fully engage the rural people in the form of agriculture desired by government. An ideologically slanted book (*The Fate of Africa, *by Martin Meredith, 2005) made the claim that Tanzania's Ujamaa villages represented a "Pol Pot lite" policy of forced agricultural collectivization leading to a rural collapse, staved off only by generous foreign aid. For this and other reasons, the government of Tanzania has been pressured to change the policy based on Ujamaa. The international banking and credit community sees the policy as an unwarranted interference in agriculture, and repeatedly threatens to withdraw credit from Tanzania. Ujamaa is a sound and humanistic policy foundation, now distorted by powerful urban and global economic forces.*

North American agriculture, superimposed from Europe alongside a quickly growing commercial and industrial economy, followed a path that destroyed the possibility of large scale population involvement in farming and destroyed the power of traditional agriculture to withstand the industrial penetration of the farming sector.

Is it possible for social workers to support the family farm in any effective way? To the extent that farm families are willing to accept the trade-offs in income and leisure, it is possible. Social workers could help organize large-scale family farm productive units on a regional basis, in which farms might share the expense of machinery, transportation, storage and other items. Machinery co-operatives have been successful. Joint contracting for seeding and harvesting may also be successful areas of co-operation.

Some religious farm colonies — like the Hutterites, Amish, Quakers and others — have developed valuable techniques in sharing to save the structures and values of farm life. Great caution is advised, however, because no romantic notion about the desirability of communal life can be imposed on people who do not have the will or means to make it work. Religious and other types of communes have strong ideological bases and usually a long tradition behind them. However, the methods and techniques used in such colonies could be instructive.

The best resources will likely be identified by rural people themselves, and the social worker probably will learn more than he or she can teach. What the worker can do, however, is enable people concerned about the survival of the family farm to share their ideas and make available to each other whatever help they can provide. The social worker may be the only person available to do such work.

The political role

Social workers typically stay away from overt political roles in urban society. It is therefore not surprising that such a question rarely occurs even in rural practice. Since social workers do not usually work as independent agents, but rather for agencies or government, their presence in rural areas has political implications. They are often regarded as carriers and imposers of policy stemming from elsewhere. Their presence is a result of the legal obligation assumed by most countries to provide some level of equitable access to services, regardless of where one resides. This legal obligation is political as well; the central government decides there is value in extending these services to expand its base of political support, to aid the casualties of development, and to encourage people to remain in rural areas.

Most obvious are those services aimed at the most vulnerable — the old, the sick, the poor; less obvious are those services aimed at the average person — health, education, etc. The social worker — sent from the city to deliver his or her part of these services — arrives with the requirement that people on the farms submit to industrialized processes to receive services. For example, to get financial assistance, farmers must order their economic lives according to standards set by industrial society. In practice this means the social worker totes up assets and potential income as if the farm were run as a business on the industrial model.

How much service an area receives is usually determined by the ability of the region to pay taxes, or by the extent to which natural resources can be extracted. Too frequently a social worker finds that rural people view the worker's entry into a region as a prelude to development for someone else's gain. Such suspicions cannot help but colour the social worker's relationship with potential clients. Social work also suffers a measure of opprobrium because the social worker usually intervenes when a farm is financially unsound. In such situations the social worker is often the source of pressure on a family to change its means of earning a livelihood. The social worker, after judging that family income does not cover costs, usually suggests that the family dispose of the farm and move to the city, where salaried employment is available (which is often not the case). If family members are unable to work, a move to the city is often still recommended because health, education and other services are not available in the countryside.

When social workers take on the role of serving the central government, as generally they must by the nature of their jobs, they often serve the interests of large agribusiness as well. Forcing the sale of a small, failing farm often means it will be bought by a large firm with the capital to incorporate it into larger holdings. A failing farmer who is angered and saddened by his or her fate sees the social worker as delivering the death blow to a small farm so a bigger operator can snap it up. Thus the social worker is cast as an industrializing influence.

In a more subtle example of the political role of social work, a worker might encourage a young person to get an education in the city when there is no apparent place available near the family farm. The lack of an option allowing the young person to stay on the farm highlights again the dominance of city interests. At times, of course, it may be completely legitimate and desirable for the social worker to play this role, when the young person wishes to make such a move and when there are useful jobs available in the cities, but dislocation is usually the result.

The economic role

The economy of any agricultural area, even where advanced modern farms dominate, is relatively simple. Production brings income, which is partially used for further production. If we can use the terms of liberal (or bourgeois) economics, there is a much smaller "multiplier effect" in agricultural communities than in urban industrial areas; that is, money invested in production creates far less economic activity than it does in the city.

In cities there is a higher multiplier effect because wages earned from working go to buy groceries, clothing, housing and other goods, and the store owners, house builders and others spend that money again on their own necessities, while services like sewerage, water and telephones are provided from both profits and taxes. The money is thus used again and again, and taxed again and again, before it finally leaves the urban community; economic activity and accelerated use of money are enhanced. In liberal economic theory such movement of money creates a climate in which economic activity increases beyond the actual flow of money from person to person.

In most North American agricultural communities, governments initiate services in an effort to build the "infrastructure" that will increase the multiplier effect of local economic activity. Social workers are not normally paid directly by their clients; their salaries are paid by the government. This transfers money to the rural community. The presence of social workers and other service personnel requires new buildings, more cars, more shops, and thus the multiplier effect grows. (It should be noted that, overall, there is a large net transfer of surplus value from the country to the city.)

The arrival of services to a rural community also increases the demand for higher levels of more complex services — recreation, libraries, cultural activities as well as wider varieties of goods. Each step of this process expands the level of economic intervention. Urban-designed products, competition among these products and regulations concerning them are imposed on the rural economy and can have both good and bad effects. The social worker has an important job to do in recognizing which interests are being served. The growth of the service sector has another less recognized effect. Bank financing of a local building industry becomes possible on a larger scale than would be the case without the presence of government or the service agency. By creating a market for office and storage space, the service industries encourage the building of offices, apartments, warehousing and other facilities, which require investment. Whether government or private industry is behind the construction, contractors usually finance the project through local banks, thus putting into circulation local money that would otherwise be invested elsewhere. The savings of local farm people are utilized and earn interest, the local economy taking on elements that look more and more like those of the industrial centres. Higher interest is earned from commercial construction and from the production of such goods as machinery than can be earned from investment in agricultural production.

Social work as an institution and as a body of knowledge and skills has no overt policy of either favouring or opposing the substructure of an area. It is part of the overall economic institutional umbrella and works alongside others in the penetration of the industrial state into rural areas.

For a time, I was a planner in the field of social programming in northern Saskatchewan. Federal and provincial governments were negotiating funding of these programs. Many groups of citizens and civil servants, aware of this pattern of development, were involved in long discussions about how to plan economic development. The building of an infrastructure containing all the elements of a regular (read "industrial") economy was seen as desirable by the majority of workers and was presented as background policy material for the inter-governmental negotiations. Documents from all over North America, and elsewhere, used the same logic and rationale for development strategy.

Helping activities in groups

It is difficult to engage agricultural people in group sessions designed to change behaviour. For reasons noted earlier, the head of the farm family is highly individualistic and used to "ruling the roost." Wives and children — though vital to the running of the farm and though respected for their traditional roles — are hardly "equal" to the patriarch's rule. Agricultural society engendered not only privately owned property and privately owned means of production, but also the "owned person." Historically slaves, wives, children and other dependants were legally under the direction and protection of the landowner. To this day the remnants of that legal system exist in marriage law in North America, most of Europe and in a number of developing areas where European law was imposed. Indigenous law frequently provided parallels that could be distorted by the European colonizers and then used to establish support for the new laws. Children likewise came under the umbrella of parental rule, and their lives were, and are still, subject to direct control by the parent until the age of adulthood.

With wives, children and slaves firmly under his control, the owner could resolve troublesome relationships by fiat. Any wife or child who attempted to escape was ordered by law back to the master. Other owners in the community were unlikely to object to this state of affairs, since they enjoyed the same privileges. The state and the police were at the beck and call of the owners to put down rebellious slaves or to retrieve errant wives or children. Social problems were often solved by force.

Modern agricultural society has mellowed somewhat in its approach to social problems. The social programs of industrial society, and the reforms wrested from the owning class by organized workers, have been extended to some degree to agricultural workers. At the same time agriculture has provided the setting within which many issues particularly surrounding the rights of women have been identified in recent years, such as farm property settlements after marriage breakup. Rural property and inheritance struggles, having a longer history in law, provide good potential for contests in court. Yet this potential is complicated because wives and children often do not have independent means of support should they try to end a farm relationship. They do not have the bargaining powers their industrial counterparts possess. Because rural community services dealing with these issues are almost non-existent, rural women and children usually have nowhere to turn for help in their struggles for change. The rural church provides further ideological support for law and custom by preaching the virtues of the dependent status of women. Distances, the difficulties of communication, and the lack of bargaining power of those most likely to suffer in their social relationships make the success of helping activities in groups unlikely.

Those who have accepted the possibility of moving to urban centres are most likely to form groups for the purpose of social change. Group work may be designed to help people change over to work related to the industrial economy. Those prepared to move to town are often encouraged by social workers to take part in "life skills" training designed to help them fit into the industrial work mould, into the social life of towns, into the economy of the city. Those group activities, then, are designed to make it possible for the people involved to make good their escape from agricultural life.

Groups organized for social change are quite different from groups that come together for social contact, recreation, religion or common interest. Social change groups aimed at changing personal behaviour, changing social functioning, or political and economic change are rarities in rural areas. There are exceptions, of course, and these are dealt with mainly in the following section on organizing in rural areas. The barriers noted above clearly illustrate this difference. In rural areas, unlike city centres, there are few groups which meet to talk about marital problems; few groups are made up of delinquent teenagers, drug users, alcoholics or people with emotional or psychological problems. Personal problems remain isolated with the individual to a far greater extent than is true of city dwellers. It may be that lack of staff assigned to helping people in groups in rural areas is the major reason for the lack of group activity. Others have suggested, wrongly, that such problems occur less often in rural areas. However, beyond the lack of social service programs, other reasons can be cited.

Pure logistics present major barriers. In urban centres, among tens of thousands of people living close together, travel is not a major problem, communications are relatively easy. Ideal treatment or therapeutic groups number somewhere between five and fifteen people. To assemble that many people in a rural setting requires participants to travel great distances. Contact between meetings is prohibitively expensive and time-consuming. The long working hours of farm families also deter people from joining groups. Though the Internet and other telecommunications provide some opportunity for group contact, much of the process of group therapy relies on direct, personal contact during which facial expression, body language and peer interchanges can be experienced first hand, with appropriate interventions by the social group worker.

The best way to establish a helping group is to use social formations already in existence, such as those in rural churches, grange organizations, producers' cooperatives and women's organizations. Many of these groups actually formed as self-help groups and are willing to define their purposes broadly.

Organizing in rural areas

One rule of thumb has been learned by rural organizers: rural agricultural people do not like to organize against their neighbours.

Rural people depend on each other in times of crisis far more than urban "cliff dwellers" do, and they generally avoid clashes with each other that may lead to divisions. To lobby against the rural council for road improvements is to affront the neighbour down the road or the person who issues grain permits. If close associates are alienated, you are left without friends or colleagues. For an agriculturist to organize against an outsider is a different story. Let a community issue grow out of an action by a city dweller, a business man or the government, and the farmers mobilize themselves with enthusiasm, regardless of the weather, bad roads and milking the cows.

The social worker must be sensitive to those issues important to agricultural people and not project preconceived notions of social change onto his or her clients. The individual property owner will, for instance, respond to any action which affects property rights, the ability to produce or the ability to market. The social worker may discover these issues by rather indirect routes. Social benefits like medicare, for example, may not directly affect the cash income of the farm family, but do defray medical costs for the relatively large families that, until recently at least, were characteristic of most agricultural areas. Non-property owners may have an interest in amenities like housing, recreation facilities, entertainment and school buses for their children.

Potent issues in North American farming communities range over railway abandonment, corporate farming, foreign land ownership, freight rates and current market prices for livestock and produce. However, there are issues common to rural people here and abroad. In many developing nations the "green revolution" is controversial; in North America many high technology, chemically intensive methods are under attack because of their health and ecological effects. But many Mexican and Asian peasants object to the green revolution because it requires expensive irrigation equipment, fertilizers and heavy equipment which the small landholder cannot afford. Another issue concerns the crops rural people market. They are ruled by the big North American agriculture and food companies who can dictate the kinds of crops to be grown in developed countries. Third World peasants who used to produce food for their own consumption now grow coffee and strawberries for the North American, Japanese and European luxury markets, while North American farmers grow the staples as well as meat products for a relatively high-priced market. For entirely different reasons the average farmer in both developed and underdeveloped countries may object to the expensive high technology, chemically intensive farming methods, but are forced into using them by falling prices and fierce competition from other parts of the globe. Their interests, though parallel, are separated by distance, communications problems, and often downright mystification by governments and others with vested interests in continuing agriculture in its current directions.

An old film produced in the 1950s by the Shell Oil company offers a revealing example of organizing to change agricultural practices. Borgo a Mozzano shows how an organizer employed by the company came to this rugged area in northern Italy and encouraged, by example and expertise, the growing of hybrid corn which yielded more than double the traditional maize crop of the region. Roads from the small hill towns to the big market centres were built. Diversification into commercial cheese making and the marketing of olives, fruit, wine and other products drew the local people into social and economic development, and into

*different farming methods, such as extensive fertiliz-
ing and the use of pesticides and herbicides.*

*After the film was made, the people stopped grow-
ing the new corn because they did not like its different taste or dough-making consistency. A more funda-
mental effect of the new maize production was that it
increased the size of landholdings, forcing some people
off the land into towns and, in many cases, out of work
as well. The film, made to illustrate the process of
organizing in rural areas, did not show the eventual
outcomes, though a rural organizer must consider such
outcomes.*

Many social workers import foreign solutions to rural
problems; the programs they operate virtually impose these
foreign solutions. They come with the best of motives, often
high ideals. However, when the imported issues and solutions fail, they are dismayed. Issues like daycare, women's
liberation and welfare rights are relevant to rural people.
However, agricultural life, and the economy that sustains
it, do not generate the same approaches to these issues as
does city life. Every area has its problems, each of which is
rooted in a specific context. The social worker must resist
the temptation to define all problems according to familiar theoretical and programmatic approaches. Successful
guidelines for establishing groups in the city can seldom
be applied without significant modifications in rural settings. (Some useful guides in doing this kind of work can be
found in Training for Transformation, manual for community workers in Zimbabwe.[12])

When social workers confront conflicting pressures —
from clients, the agency and the community — they need
to protect themselves from having their judgement clouded
by these competing pressures.[13] In practice, social workers
meet conflicting pressures by basing their judgements on
agency policy, standards from the profession, the needs of

the client, and community pressure, *in that order.*[14] Rural social workers, often working alone and away from resources and supervision, need special vigilance in order to revise such standards or priorities.

Objectives of Rural Social Work

There seems to be no feasible way to exempt any rural area from industrial processes. Short of a titanic upheaval (nuclear war, natural disaster or global epidemic), industrialism dominated by capital's financial sector will proceed. Population pressure, energy needs and the basic need for accumulation of capital for industrial growth make it inevitable that rural areas will be affected. Minerals, metals and timber as well as much power/energy from rural hydro dams are essential to the industrial process.

There are times, however, when people must oppose industrial developments which affect their area, even if the community recognizes that certain developments are inexorable and may even benefit them. The issue at hand is not one of resistance, but of control, of having a voice in directing local events. There are roles for social workers in debates over rural development, roles which might involve contesting industrial encroachment and assisting the community in its defence against penetration of industrial activities into rural areas. Resisting the use of rural areas as regions for peripheral exploitation by the industrial centres is an activity which has a growing body of support. Social workers can take up issues alongside those who argue that industrial economies are ruinous to human beings and the environment. In view of ecological damage, destruction of whole peoples, war, starvation, exploitation and other results of industrial relations, the arguments carry a certain weight. To take up these issues is unusual for social workers in that this falls outside the orthodox definition of professional social work as it stands today. In rural areas, where these issues directly affect entire communities, the social worker can legitimately incorporate them into the field of problems to be addressed.

Rural social workers cannot afford the delusion that the community in which they work will be exempted from industrial pressures. It never is.

Rural areas present to social work the challenge of defining (and redefining) issues and conditions so that people, their professional resources and service personnel can work together successfully. In much the same way as social work historically began as a service to the poor, the homeless, the dispossessed and other victim groups, social work now can approach issues that are uniquely rural and take steps to solve "new" problems.

What kind of issues are these?

Many have already been suggested earlier in this book, but a profusion of additional rural issues and conditions exist which lend themselves to social work intervention. Should aboriginal peoples be assimilated into, accommodated by or excluded from the industrial economy? (The previously popular option of exterminating them is no longer credible.[1]) Should rural technical jobs be filled by trained people from the cities, or should rural people themselves be trained and educated, even if it takes longer and may be more expensive? Should rural people be encouraged to vacate the land and move to the cities, or should programs support land tenure and offer more security? What transportation and communication policies are necessary to support the various options open to rural people? How can social workers attain the same level of resources and organization for rural areas as now exists in urban regions? Can technology offer solutions to problems created by scarcity of resources in rural areas? Some writers believe so.[2]

There is a virtually endless list of concerns which offer constructive challenges for rural social workers; all are defined by the particularities of each region and its people. The generalist approach to social work put forth earlier gives a rural social worker admirable tools to approach the issues and to help resolve them. The analytical and theoretical materials suggested provide a means for isolating the issues and ordering them. They also provide ideas and possible procedures for dealing with them.

Social work rests on one basic, undeniable premise: change is possible and necessary. Social work means change. The social worker will have to respond to the changes that will come to rural areas. In the process social work itself will change. I hope that in doing so it will draw inspiration from roots laid down many years ago.

In approaching the end of this book, this comment by Donald D. Weiss seems appropriate:

> *The development of the human powers, of the totality of human culture, must be considered a process whereby human beings become ever more able to assimilate purposefully the material environment, to transform "brute nature" into rational-intentional forms. Human culture has advanced insofar as the members of our species have literally extended their sensory-motor wherewithal, by making what was at one time mere nature into instruments wherein new sensory-motor talents can be exercised. In the (historically) first instance, the human powers were delimited by the equipment that belongs to the human body: sense organs, fingers, etc. Such powers were not, of course, insignificant; but insofar as the members of our species were restricted to such a meager physical means of interacting with their environment, their talents clearly could not be significantly more impressive than those of "the lower animals."*
>
> *By overcoming the purely "objective existence" of nature, by transforming it into physical apparatus dir-*

ectly subservient to our will, we have been able to sub-
due and to comprehend an initially hostile and mys-
terious environment. A pointed stick becomes a hoe:
thus, and only thus, is the way opened to agriculture
and hence, finally, on the more theoretical level, to
botany. We learn to control fire: not merely to warm
ourselves, but also, in time, to transform substances
into more useful substances, this being the practical
presupposition of chemistry. And so on ... Theory
must inevitably contribute to the production of human
existence on a higher material plane, if it itself is not
to be stultified.[3]

A 1993 postscript to this quotation, which I still hold to:
Since selecting that piece so many years ago, I have had several colleagues comment on its apparent lack of consciousness of the environmental emergency we all now face. Surely
a rural human service worker must be closer to some realization that the land is finite, the air, earth and water cannot take any more interventions by human beings. A rural
service worker must be closer to this realization than, for
instance, urban dwellers. However, I cannot take the avenue
of the "deep ecologists" who say we must return to the state
in which human beings harvest only what the earth and the
waters produce. I think we are beyond that possibility.

At the same time, I have no faith that disembodied,
socially disconnected technology will find a way to satisfy
human wants and needs without destroying everything in
its path. An ecologically sound technology will only save us
if human interventions make possible the political choices
for such a technology. My own sense is that such a politics
waits to be invented, combining aspects of party politics,
extra-parliamentary politics, social and justice movement
politics and various other forces that only make their presence known in the great cataclysms of history. I think such

a cataclysm is not too far off, but I can't say what form it will take, obviously.

Many attempts to create an exit from the environmentally destructive path we are on were met by the great forces of inertia in global social affairs. Neither natural disasters (human made or otherwise) nor logical discussion of the scientific and human possibilities turned us from that path.

In the meantime, humanity as it now exists will just have to try to transform the "rational-intentional forms" we now have into better ones which can serve humankind with equality and justice, while at the same time not damaging the foundation of resources upon which we all perch. It will be a struggle.

In fact, things look worse for rural people. Energy companies, largely unrestrained by rules, monitoring or enforcement, adopted a method called "hydraulic fracturing (fracking)" for extracting natural gas from deep layers of shale. In many instances, the highly pressurized water and chemical entered ground water, threatening the supply for humans, animals and plants. Other companies ramped up their search for places to store (actually dump) nuclear wastes from power generators. Naturally, the areas selected are rural locations. In both cases, the corporations offer rural people money — as little as possible — to convince them to accept fracking and storage of nuclear wastes. Issues like water access and purity, air quality and control over land and other property are thus on the table.

Notes

Preface

1. Southern Regional Education Board, Task Force on Rural Practice, "Statement of Educational Objectives," 130-6th St. S.W., Atlanta, GA, January 1972.

2. See, for instance, Ronald K. Green and Stephen A. Webster, *Social Work in Rural Areas: Preparation and Practice,* University of Tennessee School of Social Work, Knoxville, TN, 1976; Leon H. Ginsberg, *Social Work in Rural Communities,* Council on Social Work Education, 345 E. 46th St., New York, 1976; H. Wayne Johnson (Ed.), *Rural Human Services,* F.E. Peacock, Itasca, IL, 1980; and O. William Farley et al. (Eds.), *Rural Social Work Practice,* Free Press/Collier Macmillan, New York, 1982.

3. See Davis, Benjamin Marshall, *The Rural School as a Community Center,* University of Chicago Press, Chicago, 1911; Social Science Research Council (USA), Advisory Committee on Social and Economic Research in Agriculture, *Research in Rural Social Work: Scope and Method,* New York, Social Science Research Council, 1932; Di Franco, Joseph, *Extension Publications* from Interamerican Institute of Agricultural Sciences, Turialba, Costa Rica, 1960; Ehrenreich, Barbara and John, *The Cultural Crisis of Modern Medicine,* Monthly Review Press, New York, 1979; Lund, Finn Bjornar (Ed.), *Social Work Education and Practice in Rural Areas in North Norway,* Papers presented at Second Inter-University Consortium for International Social Development, Brighton, UK, August, 1982.

4. Dr. Doug Elias, an anthropologist colleague currently at the University of Lethbridge in Alberta, Canada.

1. Introduction

1. Vicente Navarro, *Medicine Under Capitalism,* Prodist (Neale Watson Academic Publications), New York, 1976.

2. Michael Tigar and Madeleine Levy, *Law and the Rise of Capitalism,* Monthly Review Press, New York, 1977.

3. Harold L. Wilensky and Charles N. LeBeaux, *Industrial Society and Social Welfare,* New York Free Press, New York, 1965.

See also Gerald Handel, *Social Welfare in Western Society*, Random House, New York, 1982; Ian Gough, *The Political Economy of the Welfare State*, Macmillan, London, 1979; John Carrier and Ian Kendall, "The development of welfare states — The production of plausible accounts," *Journal of Social Policy*, 6 (3), 1977, pp. 271–290; Allan Moscovitch and Glen Drover, *Inequality: Essays on the Political Economy of Social Welfare*, University of Toronto Press, Toronto, 1981; Claus Offe, *Contradictions of the Welfare State*, Hutchinson, London, 1984.

4. For an excellent antidote to such vulgarizing, see Ellen Meiksins Wood in John Saville and Leo Panitch, *Socialist Register, 1990: The Retreat of the Intellectuals*, Merlin, London, 1990.

5. Peter Farb, *Man's Rise to Civilization: As Shown by the Indians of North America From Primeval Times to the Coming of the Industrial State*, E.P. Dutton and Co., New York, 1968.

6. See Terry Eagleton, *The Illusions of Postmodernism*, Basil Blackwell, Cambridge, UK, 1996; David Harvey, *The Condition of Postmodernity*, Blackwell, Cambridge, MA, USA, 1990; Ellen Meiksins Wood and John Bellamy Foster (Eds.), *In Defense of History: The Postmodern Agenda*, Monthly Review Press, New York, 1997; and John Sanbonmatsu, *The Postmodern Prince: Critical Theory, Left Strategy, and the Making of a New Political Subject*, Monthly Review Press, New York, 2004.

2. Economic phases and helping relationships

1. Marshall Sahlins, "The Original Affluent Society," in his *Stone-Age Economics*, Aldine-Atherton, Chicago, 1972.

2. The debate about the division of labour between men and women enters here, but it has been resolved well enough by others. See Eleanor Burke Leacock, *Myths of Male Dominance*, Monthly Review Press, New York, 1981, esp. pp. 310–316. See also Leacock's introduction to Friedrich Engels' *Origin of the Family, Private Property and the State*, Progress Books, Moscow, 1948.

3. Benjamin Lee Whorf, *Language, Thought and Reality*, MIT Press, Cambridge, 1956, pp. 57–64 and 134–159; and David G. Mandelbaum (Ed.), *Selected Writings of Edward Sapir*, University of California Press, San Francisco, 1949, pp. 432–462. Sapir seems to have adopted this view in his later writings, but not in earlier texts.

4. Peter Farb, op. cit.

5. For especially insightful treatment of this material, see Kathleen Gough, "The Origin of the Family," in Rayna Reiter (Ed.), *Toward an Anthropology of Women*, Monthly Review Press, New York, 1975, pp. 51–76. See also Karen Sacks, "Engels Revisited:

Women, the Organization of Production and Private Property," in Rayna Reiter, op. cit., pp. 211–234.

6. Samir Amin has telling criticisms of this "West-centred" interpretation of historic events. He sees British "feudalism" as a primitive form of tributary society which, because of its peripheral status in the world economic system of the time, was the first local system capable of transforming itself into nascent capitalism. See Samir Amin, *Class and Nation, Historically and in the Current Crisis*, Monthly Review Press, New York, 1980.

7. R.H. Tawney, *Religion and the Rise of Capitalism*, P. Smith, Gloucester, MA, 1962.

8. See E.K. Hunt, *Property and Prophets* (2nd Ed.), Harper and Row, New York, 1975, especially the chapter "The Transition from Feudalism to Capitalism," p. 15ff. Also, Peter Mathias, *The First Industrial Nation: An Economic History of Britain 1700-1914*, Methuen, London, 1969.

9. See Frances Fox Piven and Richard Cloward, *Regulating the Poor* (2nd Ed.), Vintage Books, New York, 1993, p. 8ff.

10. Passages through economic phases toward the welfare state are treated by Mike Fitzgerald in Unit 3 of *Introduction to Welfare: The Iron Fist and the Velvet Glove*, Open University Press, London, 1978, pp. 91–132.

11. Recent findings and studies indicate no sharp break between foraging and agriculture or husbandry of the environment. Calvin Martin in *Keepers of the Game* (University of California Press, San Francisco, 1978) offers an unromanticized account of remote peoples in Canada ensuring that hunting, fishing, trapping and gathering environments were not damaged by overuse or abuse, and how gatherers replaced, by allowing fallow periods, the game they had taken. In many parts of the North, even now, game trapping and fishing quotas are based more on ancient aboriginal practices than on "scientific" biological data found by experts. "Domestication" takes on a somewhat enhanced meaning when we consider this careful orientation to the laws of nature and people being only one part of a whole which requires respect and balance. The relationship between people and their environment appears more calculated and purposive than industrial societies are often willing to admit. See a crucial new addition to the relevant world literature – Mazoyer, Marcel and Laurence Roudart, *A History of World Agriculture: From the Neolithic Age to the Current Crisis*, Monthly Review Press, New York, 2014.

12. For details on underdevelopment, see especially Samir Amin, *Unequal Development: An Essay on the Social Formations of Peripheral Capitalism*, Monthly Review Press, New York, 1974. See also Samir Amin, *Imperialism and Unequal Develop-*

ment, Monthly Review Press, New York, 1977, a series of essays on aspects of this question. How this relates to welfare in general is found in Vicente Navarro, "The Crisis of the International Capitalist Order, Class Struggle and the Welfare State," in *Catalyst,* No. 7, 1980. A useful early source is Andre Gunder Frank, *Capitalism and Underdevelopment in Latin America,* Monthly Review Press, New York, 1967. See also his *Critique and Anti-Critique,* Praeger, New York, 1984.

13. See Cheryl Payer, *The Debt Trap: The International Monetary Fund and the Third World,* Monthly Review Press, New York, 1974. Also John Loxley, *Debt and Disorder: External Financing for Development,* Westview Press/North-South Institute, Boulder, CO, 1986.

14. Guillermo O'Donnell, "Reflections on the Pattern of Change in the Bureaucratic-Authoritarian State," *Latin American Research Review,* Vol. XIII, No.1, 1978. For some challenging alternatives, see Nils Christie, "Crime Control as Industry: A Conversation with David Cayley," CBC *Ideas,* March 10, 17, and 24, 1993 (transcripts available from CBC Toronto - http://www.cbc.ca).

3. Social Work In Industrial Society

1. See Harold L. Wilensky and Charles N. LeBeaux, op. cit.; Karl De Schweinitz, *England's Road to Social Security,* A.S. Barnes (Perpetua), New York, 1943; and Andrew Armitage, *Social Welfare in Canada,* McClelland and Stewart, Toronto, 1975, esp. pp. 213–220; Dennis Guest, *The Emergence of Social Security in Canada,* University of British Columbia Press, Vancouver, 1980; Gerald Handel, *Social Welfare in Western Society,* Random House, New York, 1982; Brian Wharf (Ed.), *Social Work and Social Change in Canada,* McClelland and Stewart, Toronto, 1990.

2. Eli Zaretsky, *Capitalism, the Family and Personal Life,* Pluto Press, London, 1976.

3. Ken Collier, "Rural Casework," *Canadian Welfare Journal,* Vol. 42, Nos. 3 and 4, September 1966. See also *Human Services in the Rural Environment (HSITRE),* a journal produced by a number of different university faculties of social work through the years.

4. Generalist Practice: The Best Option

1. Reported in Ian Westbury, Bernece K. Simon and John Korbelik, *The Generalist Program: Description and Evaluation,* School of Social Service Administration, University of Chicago Press, Chicago, 1973, pp. 202–217.

2. Allen Pincus and Anne Minahan, *Social Work Practice: Model and Method*, F.E. Peacock, Itasca, IL, 1973, p. xiii.

3. See Allen Pincus and Anne Minahan, op. cit., for early discussion of the approach as one choice that could be developed out of their writing. Two other texts stand out on this approach: Joseph Anderson, *Social Work Methods and Processes*, Wadsworth Publishing Company, Belmont, CA, 1981 (now unfortunately out of print), and Louise Johnson, *Social Work Practice: A Generalist Approach*, 4th Ed., Allyn and Bacon, Boston, 1992.

5. Social Work In Remote Communities

1. Emmanuel Terray, *Marxism and 'Primitive' Societies*, Monthly Review Press, New York, 1972; Maurice Bloch, *Marxist Analysis and Social Anthropology*, Association of Social Anthropologists, Halsted Press, New York, 1975; and Pierre-Philippe Rey, *Les Alliances des Classes. Sur l'Articulation des Modes de Production. Suivi de Materialisme, Historique et Lutte de Classes*, Maspero, Paris, 1973.

2. Robert Davis and Mark Zannis, *The Genocide Machine in Canada*, Black Rose Books, Montreal, 1973; and Bruce Johansen and Roberto Maestas, *Wasi'Chu: The Continuing Indian Wars*, Monthly Review Press, New York, 1979.

3. *Saskatoon Star-Phoenix*, October 31, 1991.

4. Marshall Sahlins, *Stone-Age Economics*, Aldine-Atherton Press, Chicago, 1972.

5. John F. Bryde, *Modern Indian Psychology*, Institute of Indian Studies, University of South Dakota, Vermillion, SD, 1971. This book contains some material that may be open to challenge, so use it with caution.

6. Thomas Szasz, *The Myth of Mental Illness*, Harper and Row, New York, 1974; and John and Barbara Ehrenreich, *The Cultural Crisis of Modern Medicine*, Monthly Review Press, New York, 1979. See also virtually anything by R.D. Laing.

7. See William Ryan, *Blaming the Victim*, Pantheon, New York, 1971.

8. Irving Hallowell, "Ojibwa World View and Medicine," in Iago Goldston (Ed.), *Man's Image in Medicine and Anthropology*, Monograph IV, Institute of Social and Historical Medicine, New York Academy of Medicine, International University Press, New York, 1963.

9. See, in addition, Heather Robertson, *Reservations Are For Indians*, James Lewis and Samuel, Toronto, 1970; Rosemary Sarri, Maeda Galinsky, Paul Glasser, Sheldon Siegel and Robert Vinter, "Diagnosis in Group Work," in Robert Vinter, *Readings in Group*

Work Practice, Campus Publishers, Ann Arbor, MI, 1967, pp. 50–51.

6. Social Work In Rural Agricultural Societies

1. This emergence from foraging to early agriculture is described with great clarity in Friedrich Engels, *Origin of the Family, Private Property and the State*, Progress Books, Moscow, 1948. See especially pp. 29–74.

2. Samir Amin, "Self-Reliance and the New International Economic Order," *Monthly Review*, Vol. 29, No. 3, July/August 1977. See, as well, note 12 for further reference on this topic. Of great use are James Petras, *Critical Perspectives on Imperialism and Social Class in the Third World*, Monthly Review Press, New York, 1978; John Saul and Craig Heron, *Imperialism, Nationalism and Canada*, New Hogtown Press and Between The Lines, Toronto and Kitchener, 1977; Cheryl Payer, op. cit.; Ken Collier, "Underdevelopment in Saskatchewan," unpublished paper (mimeo), Faculty of Social Work, University of Regina, Regina, SK, 1981.

3. Alan Mairson, "65760 Not Quite Utopia (Zip USA)," *National Geographic*, Vol. 208, No. 2, August 2005, pp. 114–118.

4. R.H. Tawney, op. cit.

5. For instance, see Josephine C. Brown, *The Rural Community and Social Casework*, Family Welfare Association of America, New York, 1933.

6. Carol L. Schafer, "This Rural Social Work," *The Survey*, Vol. 75, May 1939, p. 138; and Wilma Van Dusseldorp, "The Development of Social Agencies in Rural Communities," *The Family*, Vol. 19, March 1933, p. 20.

7. Josephine Strode, "Rural Social Workers Do Everything," *The Survey*, Vol. 74, October 1938, p. 308; and A.A. Amisle, "Training for Rural Social Work," *Sociology and Social Research*, July 22, 1938, p. 538. The history of this interlude in American social work has been recorded by Emilia Martinez-Brawley, "History and Reminiscence in Rural Social Work: Lessons for Training and Retraining," in Edward B. Buxton (Ed.), *Training and Retraining for Effective Practice: Second National Institute of Social Work in Rural Areas Reader*, University of Wisconsin, Madison, 1978, pp. 107–120; and Emilia Martinez-Brawley (Ed.), *Pioneer Efforts in Rural Social Welfare: Firsthand Views Since 1908*, Pennsylvania State University Press, Philadelphia, 1980. See *Human Services in the Rural Environment (HSITRE)*, University of Wisconsin, Madison, published 1976–1978. Since then, *HSITRE* has moved through several university publishers.

8. Les Senner, Associate Professor of Social Work, University of Regina, Community Education Centre, Prince Albert, SK. Mr. Senner formerly worked in rural mental health and on Indian reserves in Montana and South Dakota.

9. I highly recommend Friedrich Engels, *Origin of the Family, Private Property and the State*. See works cited in note 7 above.

10. See John Warnock, *Profit Hungry: The Food Industry in Canada*, New Star Books, Vancouver, 1979. See also Don Mitchell, *The Politics of Food*, James Lorimer, Toronto, 1975; R. Alex Sim, *Land and Community: The Crisis in Canada's Countryside*, University of Guelph Press, Guelph, ON, 1988.

11. See Jack Grey, "China's Economic Strategy," in Alec Nove (Ed.), *Socialist Economics*, Penguin, New York, 1972, pp. 491–510; and Claude Njimba, "Social Work Curriculum for Rural Areas in Developing Countries," unpublished Master's thesis, School of Social Work, McGill University, Montreal, 1976. An unusually valuable film, *A Fair Share of What Little We Have*, British Broadcasting Corporation, London, 1972, on Tanzania's health system.

12. Anne Hope and Sally Timmel, *Training for Transformation: A Handbook for Community Workers* (3 vols.), Mambo Press, Gweru, Zimbabwe, 1984.

13. Rosemary Sarri et al, "Diagnosis in Group Work," in Robert Vinter, op. cit.

14. Andrew Billingsley, "Bureaucratic and Professional Orientation Patterns in Social Casework," *Social Service Review*, No. 38, December 1964, pp. 400–407.

7. Objectives of Rural Social Work

1. See in this regard Hans Koning, *Columbus: His Enterprise*, 2nd Ed., Monthly Review Press, New York, 1992. See also various issues of *Akwesasne Notes*, an award-winning aboriginal and natural people's newspaper published by the Mohawk Nation, Rooseveltown, New York, especially the October 1977 issue; and Dee Brown, *Bury My Heart at Wounded Knee*, Bantam Books, New York, 1971; and Robert Davis and Mark Zannis, op. cit.

2. Jo Ann R. Coe and Goutham M. Menon (Eds.), *Computers and Information Technologies in Social Work*, Haworth Press, New York, 1999. Their authors discuss several applications in rural social work and other service professions.

3. Donald D. Weiss, "The Philosophy of Engels Vindicated," *Monthly Review*, Vol. 28, No. 3, January, 1977, pp. 23–25.

Bibliography

Akwesasne Notes, Newspaper of the Mohawk Nation, Roosevel-town, New York, various editions.

Amin, Samir, *Accumulation World Scale: A Critique of the Theory of Underdevelopment*, Monthly Review Press, New York, 1974.

— *Class and Nation, Historically and in the Current Crisis*, Monthly Review Press, New York, 1980.

— *Imperialism and Unequal Development*, Monthly Review Press, New York, 1977.

— "Self-Reliance and the New International Economic Order," *Monthly Review*, Vol. 29, No. 3, July/August 1977.

— Unequal Development: An Essay on the Social Formations of Peripheral Capitalism, Monthly Review Press, New York, 1976.

Amisle, A.A., "Training for Rural Social Work," *Sociology and Social Research*, July 1938.

Anderson, Joseph, *Social Work Methods and Processes*, Wadsworth Publishing Co., Belmont, CA, 1981.

Armitage, Andrew, *Social Welfare in Canada*, McClelland and Stewart, Toronto, 1975.

Balicki, Asen, *Yesterday-Today: The Netsilik Eskimo*, National Film Board of Canada, Ottawa, 1971 (film).

— *The Eskimo: Fight For Life*, (film) National Film Board of Canada, Ottawa, 1971.

Ballantyne, Phillip, et al, *Aski Puko: The Land Alone*, Federation of Saskatchewan Indians, Prince Albert, SK, 1976.

Bielawski, Ellen, "Inuit Indigenous Knowledge and Science in the Arctic," *Northern Perspectives*, 20 (1), Summer 1992, Canadian Arctic Resources Committee, Ottawa.

Billingsley, Andrew, "Bureaucratic and Professional Orientation Patterns Social Casework," *Social Service Review*, No. 38, December 1964.

Bloch, Maurice, *Marxist Analysis and Social Anthropology*, Association of Social Anthropologists, Halsted Press, New York, 1975.

Bollman, Ray D. (Ed.), *Rural and Small Town Canada*, Toronto, Educational Publishing, Toronto, 1992.

Brown, Dee, *Bury My Heart at Wounded Knee*, Bantam Books, New York, 1971.

Brown, Josephine, *The Rural Community and Social Casework*, Family Welfare Association of America, New York, 1933.

Bryde, John F., *Modern Indian Psychology*, Institute of Indian Studies, University of South Dakota, Vermillion, SD, 1971.

Carrier, John and Ian Kendall, "The development of welfare states — The production of plausible accounts," *Journal of Social Policy*, (3), 1977.

Chambers, Robert, *Rural Development: Putting the Last First*, Longman, New York, 1983.

Coe, Jo Ann R. and Goutham. M. Menon (Eds.) *Computers and Information Technologies in Social Work*, Haworth, New York, 1999.

Collier, Ken, "Rural Casework," *Canadian Welfare Journal*, Vol. 42, Nos. 3 and 4, September 1966.

— "Underdevelopment in Saskatchewan," unpublished paper (mimeo), Faculty of Social Work, University of Regina, Regina, SK, 1981.

— "Social Spending and Underdevelopment in the Advanced Periphery: Mid-Wales and Northern Saskatchewan," unpublished thesis, University of Wales, Swansea, 1991.

Dabby, Layla, "Northern Exposure," *Globe and Mail*, Toronto, August 27, 2005.

Davenport, Joseph and Judith (Eds.), *Social Work in Rural Areas: Issues and Opportunities*, University of Wyoming Department of Social Work, Laramie, WY, 1980.

Davis, Benjamin Marshall, *The Rural School as a Community Center*, University of Chicago Press, Chicago, 1911.

Davis, Robert and Mark Zannis, *The Genocide Machine in Canada*, Black Rose Books, Montreal, 1973.

Deere, Carmen Diana and Magdalena Leon (Eds.), *Rural Women and State Policy: Feminist Perspectives on Latin American Agricultural Development*, Westview Press, Boulder, CO, 1987.

Di Franco, Joseph, *Extension Publications from Interamerican Institute of Agricultural Sciences*, Turialba, Costa Rica, 1960.

Eagleton, Terry, *The Illusions of Postmodernism*, Basil Blackwell, Cambridge, UK, 1996.

Ehrenreich, Barbara and John, *The Cultural Crisis of Modern Medicine*, Monthly Review Press, New York, 1979.

Elias, Peter Douglas (Ed.) *Northern Aboriginal Communities: Economies and Development*, Captus Press, North York, ON, 1995.

Engels, Friedrich, *Origin of the Family, Private Property and the State*, Progress Books, Moscow, 1948.

Farb, Peter, *Man's Rise to Civilization: As Shown by the Indians of North America from Primeval Times to the Coming of the Industrial State*, E.P. Dutton, New York, 1968.

Farley, O. William et al. (Eds.), *Rural Social Work Practice*, Free Press/Collier, Macmillan, New York, 1982.

Fitzgerald, Mike, *Introduction to Welfare: The Iron Fist and the Velvet Glove*, Open University Press, London, 1978.

Frank, Andre Gunder, *Capitalism and Underdevelopment in Latin America*, Monthly Review Press, New York, 1967.

— *Critique and Anti-Critique*, Praeger, New York, 1984.

Gianotten, Vera, *Methodological Notes for Evaluation*, Food and Agricultural Organization of the United Nations, Rome, 1986.

Gill, Stephen, "Globalization, Democratization and the Politics of Indifference," in Mittelman, James H., (Ed.) *Globalization: Critical Reflections*, Lynne Rienner, Boulder, CO, 1996.

Ginsberg, Leon H. (Ed.), *Social Work in Rural Communities*, Council on Social Work Education, New York, 1976.

Gough, Ian, *The Political Economy of the Welfare State*, Macmillan, London, 1979.

Gough, Kathleen (Aberle), "The Origin of the Family," in Rayna Reiter (Ed.), *Toward an Anthropology of Women*, Monthly Review Press, New York, 1975.

Great Plains Staff Training and Development for Rural Mental Health Project, *Human Services in the Rural Transition*, University of Nebraska, Lincoln, NE, 1989 (video and training package).

Green, Ronald K., and Stephen A. Webster, *Social Work in Rural Areas: Preparation and Practice*, Papers presented at 1st National Institute on Social Work in Rural Areas, July 13–16, 1976, University of Tennessee School of Social Work, Knoxville, TN, 1976.

Grey, Jack, "China's Economic Strategy," in Alec Nove (Ed.) *Socialist Economics*, Penguin, New York, 1972.

Guest, Dennis, *The Emergence of Social Security in Canada*, University of British Columbia Press, Vancouver, 1980.

Hallowell, Irving, "Ojibwa World View and Medicine," in Iago Goldston (Ed.), *Man's Image in Medicine and Anthropology*, Monograph IV, Institute of Social and Historical Medicine, International University Press, New York, 1963.

Handel, Gerald, *Social Welfare in Western Society*, Random House, New York, 1982.

Harvey, David, *The Condition of Postmodernity*, Blackwell, Cambridge, MA, 1990.

Hinton, William, *Fanshen*, Monthly Review Press, New York, 1966.

— *Shenfan: The Continuing Revolution in a Chinese Village*, Monthly Review Press, New York, 1980.

— *China: An Unfinished Battle*, Cornerstone Publications, Kharagsur, India, 2002.

— "Background Notes to *Fanshen*", available at http://www.monthlyreview.org/1003hinton.htm.

Hoagland, Marjorie, "A New Day in Rural Mental Health Services," *New Directions in Mental Health*, Publ. No. 78-690, Alcohol, Drug Abuse and Mental Health Administration, Public Health Services, Department of Health, Education and Welfare, Rockville, MD, 1978.

Hope, Anne and Sally Timmel, *Training for Transformation: A Handbook for Community Workers*, Books 1, 2 and 3, Mambo Press, Zimbabwe, 1984; available from P.O. Box 779, Gweru, Zimbabwe.

Human Services in the Rural Environment, (Journal), University of Wisconsin Press, Madison, 1976-78. Since moved to other universities, now lodged at the University of Tennesee.

Hunt, E.K., *Property and Prophets*, Harper and Row, New York, 1975.

Jenness, Diamond, "The Indians of Canada," Bulletin 65, Anthropological Series, National Museum of Canada, Ottawa, 1932.

Johansen, Bruce and Roberto Maestas, *Wasi'Chu: The Continuing Indian Wars*, Monthly Review Press, New York, 1979.

Johnson, Leo, *Poverty in Wealth*, New Hogtown Press, Toronto, 1974.

Johnson, Louise, *Social Work Practice: A Generalist Approach*, Allyn and Bacon, Boston, 1983.

Johnson, H. Wayne, *Rural Human Services*, F.E. Peacock, Itasca, IL, 1980.

Kinney, Jean, *Clinical Manual of Substance Abuse*, Mosby, St. Louis, MO, 1996.

Koning, Hans, *Columbus: His Enterprise*, Monthly Review Press, New York, 1976.

— *The Almost World*, Monthly Review Press, New York, 1974.

Laing, Ronald D., *The Politics of Experience*, Pantheon Books, New York, 1967.

Leacock, Eleanor Burke, *Myths of Male Dominance*, Monthly Review Press, New York, 1981.

Levi-Strauss, Claude, "The Story of Asdiwal," in Edmund Leach (Ed.), *The Structural Study of Myth and Totemism*, Tavistock Publications, London, 1967.

Loxley, John, *Debt and Disorder: External Financing For Development*, Westview/North-South Institute, Boulder, CO, 1986.

Lund, Finn Bjornar (Ed.), *Social Work Education and Practice in Rural Areas in North Norway*, Papers presented at Second Inter-University Consortium for International Social Development, Brighton, UK, August, 1982.

Mairson, Alan, "65760: Not Quite Utopia" (ZipUSA), *National Geographic*, Vol. 208, No. 2, August, 2005, pp. 114-118.

Mandelbaum, David G. (Ed.), *Selected Writings of Edward Sapir*, University of California Press, San Francisco, 1949.

Martin, Calvin, *Keepers of the Game*, University of California Press, San Francisco, 1978.

Martinez-Brawley, Emilia, "History and Reminiscence in Rural Social Work: Lessons for Training and Retraining," in Edward B. Buxton (Ed.), *Training and Retraining For Effective Practice: Second National Institute of Social Work in Rural Areas Reader*, University of Wisconsin, Madison, 1978.

— (Ed.), *Pioneer Efforts in Rural Social Welfare: Firsthand Views Since 1908*, Pennsylvania State University Press, Philadelphia, 1980.

Mathias, Peter, *The First Industrial Nation: An Economic History of Britain 1700-1914*, Methuen, London, 1969.

Mazoyer, Marcel and Laurence Roudart, *A History of World Agriculture: From the Neolithic Age to the Current Crisis*, Monthly Review Press, New York, 2014.

Meredith, Martin, *The Fate of Africa: From the Hopes of Freedom to the Heart of Despair: A History of 50 Years of Independence*, Public Affairs Press, London, 2005.

Mitchell, Don, *The Politics of Food*, James Lorimer, Toronto, 1975.

Naegele, Kaspar, "Modern National Societies," in Bernard Blishen et al. (Eds.), *Canadian Society — Sociological Perspectives*, Macmillan, Toronto, 1968.

National Film Board of Canada, *Promises, Promises*. 1973 (film; now available from the National Film Board of Canada on DVD as part of collections on rural life).

Navarro, Vicente, "The Crisis of International Capitalist Order, Class Struggle and the Welfare State," *Catalyst: A Socialist Journal of the Social Services*, No. 7, New York, 1980.

— *Medicine Under Capitalism*, Prodist (Neale Watson Academic Publications), New York, 1976.

Njimba, Claude, "Social Work Curriculum for Rural Areas in Developing Countries," unpublished Master's thesis, School of Social Work, McGill University, Montreal, 1976.

"Northern Residents Fear Health Threat from Creosote Applied to Homes," *Saskatoon Star-Phoenix*, October 31, 1991.

O'Donnell, Guillermo, "Reflections on the Pattern of Change in the Bureaucratic-Authoritarian State," *Latin American Research Review*, Vol. XIII, No. 1, 1978.

Offe, Claus, *Contradictions of the Welfare State*, Hutchinson, London, 1984.

Panitch, Leo. "Rethinking the Role of the States" in Mittelman, James H. (Ed.), *Globalization: Critical Reflections*, Lynne Rienner, Boulder, CO, 1996.

Payer, Cheryl, *The Debt Trap: The International Monetary Fund and the Third World*, Monthly Review Press, New York, 1974.

Petras, James, *Critical Perspectives on Imperialism and Social Class in the Third World*, Monthly Review Press, New York, 1978.

Pincus, Allen, and Anne Minahan, *Social Work Practice: Model and Method*, F.E. Peacock, Itasca, IL, 1973.

Piven, Frances Fox, and Richard Cloward, *Regulating the Poor*, Vintage Books, New York, 1971.

Porter, John, *The Vertical Mosaic: An Analysis of Social Class and Power*, University of Toronto Press, Toronto, 1965.

Pugh, Richard, *Rural Social Work*, Russell House, Lyme Regis, UK, 2000.

Reiter, Rayna, *Toward an Anthropology of Women*, Monthly Review Press, New York, 1975.

Rey, Pierre-Philippe, *Les Alliances des Classes. Sur l'Articulation des Modes de Production. Suivi de Materialisme, Historique et Lutte de Classes*, Maspero, Paris, 1973.

Robertson, Heather, *Reservations Are for Indians*, James Lewis and Samuel, Toronto, 1970.

Ryan, William, *Blaming the Victim*, Pantheon, New York, 1971.

Sacks, Karen, "Engels Revisited: Women, the Organization of Production and Private Property," in Rayna Reiter (Ed.), *Toward an Anthropology of Women*, Monthly Review Press, New York, 1975.

Saegart, Susan, J. Phillip Thompson and Mark R. Warren (Eds.), *Social Capital and Poor Communities*, Russell Sage Foundation, New York, 2001.

Sahlins, Marshall, *Stone-Age Economics*, Aldine-Atherton Press, Chicago, 1972.

Sanbonmatsu, John, *The Postmodern Prince: Critical Theory, Left Strategy, and the Making of a New Political Subject*, Monthly Review Press, New York, 2004.

Sarri, Rosemary et al., "Diagnosis in Group Work," in Robert Vinter (Ed.), *Readings in Group Work Practice*, Campus Publishers, Ann Arbor, MI, 1967.

Saul, John and Craig Heron, *Imperialism, Nationalism and Canada*, New Hogtown Press, Toronto, and Between the Lines, Kitchener, ON, 1977.

Schafer, Carol L., "This Rural Social Work," *The Survey*, Vol. 75, New York, May 1939.

Scales, T. Laine and Calvin L. Streeter (Eds.), *Rural Social Work: Building and Sustaining Community Assets*, Brooks/Cole Thompson Learning, Belmont, CA, 2004.

Sim, R. Alex, *Land and Community: The Crisis in Canada's Countryside*, University of Guelph Press, Guelph, ON, 1988.

Smith, Claudia M and Frances Maurer (Eds.), *Community Health Nursing: Theory and Practice* (2nd Ed.), Saunders Publishing, Philadelphia, 2000.

Smith, Wallis, "The Development of Underdevelopment," unpublished working paper, La Ronge, SK, 1972.

Social Science Research Council (U.S.), Advisory Committee on Social and Economic Research in Agriculture, *Research in Rural Social Work: Scope and Method*, Social Science Research Council, New York, 1932.

Strode, Josephine, "Rural Social Workers Do Everything," *The Survey*, Vol. 74, October 1938.

Szasz, Thomas, *The Myth of Mental Illness*, Harper and Row, New York, 1974.

Tawney, R.H., *Religion and the Rise of Capitalism*, P. Smith, Gloucester, MA, 1962.

Terray, Emmanuel, *Marxism and "Primitive" Societies*, Monthly Review Press, New York, 1972.

Tigar, Michael, and Madeleine Levy, *Law and the Rise of Capitalism*, Monthly Review Press, New York, 1977.

United Nations Study Group on Rural Social Development, *People in the Countryside: A Report Based on the Work of the U.N. European Study Group held at Beaumont Hall, University of Leicester, UK*, National Council of Social Services, London, 1966.

Van Dusseldorp, Wilma, "The Development of Social Agencies in Rural Communities," *The Family*, Vol. 19, March 1933.

Vanderklippe, Nathan, "Inuit Want Story of RCMP Dog Slaughter Made Public," *Globe and Mail*, Toronto, July 17, 2005.

Warnock, John, *Profit Hungry: The Food Industry in Canada*, New Star Books, Vancouver, 1979.

— *Free Trade and the New Right Agenda*, New Star Books, Vancouver, 1988.

Weiss, Donald D. "The Philosophy of Engels Vindicated," *Monthly Review*, New York, Vol. 28, No. 3, January 1977.

Westbury, Ian, Bernece K. Simon and John Korbelik, *The Gen-*

eralist Program: Description and Evaluation, School of Social Service Administration, University of Chicago Press, Chicago, 1973.

Wharf, Brian (Ed.), *Social Work and Social Change in Canada*, McClelland and Stewart, Toronto, 1990.

Whorf, Benjamin Lee, *Language, Thought and Reality*, MIT Press, Cambridge, MA, 1956.

Wilensky, Harold L., and Charles N. LeBeaux, *Industrial Society and Social Welfare*, New York Free Press, New York, 1965.

Wood, Ellen Meiksins and John Bellamy Foster (Eds.), *In Defense of History: The Postmodern Agenda*, Monthly Review Press, New York, 1997.

Zapf, Michael Kim, *Rural Social Work and its Application to the Canadian North as a Practice Setting*, Toronto University Press, Toronto, 1985.

Zaretsky, Eli, *Capitalism, the Family and Personal Life*, Pluto Press, London, 1976.

Index

CPSIA information can be obtained
at www.ICGtesting.com
Printed in the USA
FSOW01n1019260914
3155FS